New Cambridge
MATHEMATICS

■ ▲ ● **MODULE 2** ● ▲ ■

Games and mats
Teacher's handbook

■
Sue Atkinson

▲
Wendy Garrard

●
Sharon Harrison

■
Lynne McClure

▲

CAMBRIDGE
UNIVERSITY PRESS

Published by the Press Syndicate of the University of Cambridge
The Pitt Building, Trumpington Street, Cambridge CB2 1RP
40 West 20th Street, New York, NY 10011-4211, USA
10 Stamford Road, Oakleigh, Melbourne 3166, Australia

© Cambridge University Press 1995

First published 1995

Printed in Great Britain by GreenShires Print Ltd, Kettering

ISBN 0 521 47191 5

Introduction to the games

The games are designed to provide consolidation of mathematical ideas in an enjoyable way. They can also be used to encourage co-operative working and to develop powers of reasoning by thinking about strategies. References to games relevant to particular activities are given in the Teacher's resource book.

How to prepare the games

The grid on page 2 shows the base boards, sheets of cut-ups and equipment needed for each game. A plastic bag and label is provided for each one. It is a good idea to include a copy of the rules in the bag as well as the boards, cut-ups and equipment. The cut-ups should be cut along the *dashed* lines only to make cards.

To assemble the **spinners**, copy page 4, divide it into sections and cut out the small central circles. Separate the two parts of the plastic spinner. Fit the circle over the raised centre of the plastic base then push the arrow back in place.

How to use the games

The games can be used in the classroom to provide further practice or they can be sent home for children to play with their families. It is a good idea to play the games with the children in order to introduce the rules. Most boards can be used for several different games and suggestions are provided which generally increase in difficulty. Of course, the children can also make up their own rules.

Children's own games

Page 3 can be photocopied to give children the opportunity to make up their own mathematical track game. You might want to suggest a context, such as a game of racing cars or bikes, or something connected with your class topic. Wrapping paper pictures or pictures from greetings cards can be stuck onto a copy of the sheet. Encourage children to make up their own rules. Making a game is a good context in which children can explore a calculator.

Equipment given in italics is not supplied in the pack. Some non standard dice are required.
Blank dice and stickers are supplied, but you may prefer to write on a larger wooden cube.

Title	Boards	Cut-ups	Equipment	Mathematical content
Stamps	0	32 cards 2 different sheets	2 dice (1–6)	sorting 2D shape addition money
Dragon's lair	1	20 dragon fire cards $1\frac{1}{4}$ sheets 8 golden number cards $\frac{1}{2}$ sheet	2 dice (1–6) 2 each red, yellow, blue and green counters 30 orange counters *cubes, number line,* *calculator*	counting addition subtraction multiplication
Rainbow race	2 the same	0	4 dice (1–6) 2 each red, yellow, blue, green counters 20 orange counters *timer, calculator, cubes*	counting addition subtraction multiplication (ext) time
Jungle journey	1	9 cards 1 sheet	2 dice (1–6) 9 each red, yellow, blue, green counters	addition routes
Clown coconuts	1	0	2 dice (1–6) 9 each red, yellow, blue counters *red, yellow, brown cubes* *calculators, other dice*	addition subtraction multiplication division prime nos (ext)
Escape from the crocodile	1	0	2 dice (1–6) 2 red, 2 yellow counters	counting addition number bonds strategy
Robot rummy	0	40 cards $2\frac{1}{2}$ sheets	*calculator*	counting sorting and matching 2D shape
Don't block me in!	1	0	1 red, 1 blue counter 1 dice (1–6) *cubes*	strategy odd and even numbers counting
Gold diggers' island	1	40 cards 2 sheets	60 orange counters 1 red, 1 yellow, 1 blue counter dice (1–6) *calculator*	co-ordinates counting addition multiplication (ext)
Pocket money	1	0	dice (1–6) *play or real money* 1 each red, yellow, blue, green counter	money up to £1 giving change days of the week
Palm tree pennies	2 the same	0	dice (1–6) spinner (1p, 1p, 1p, 2p, 2p, 5p, 10p, 20p) *play or real money*	money to 20p recognition of coins exchange of coins
Cross the magic river	1	6 cards $\frac{1}{4}$ sheet	spinner (3, 4, 5, 6) spinner (triangle, quadrilateral, pentagon, hexagon) 12 each red and yellow counters	counting 2D shape strategy
Party food	2 the same	32 cards 2 sheets	spinner ($\frac{1}{4}, \frac{1}{4}, \frac{1}{2}, \frac{1}{2}, \frac{3}{4}, \frac{3}{4}$ in shapes not nos) spinner ($\frac{1}{4}, \frac{1}{4}, \frac{1}{2}, \frac{1}{2}, \frac{3}{4}, \frac{3}{4}$)	halves, quarters addition
Turtle money trail	1	32 cards 2 sheets 8 turtles	dice (1–6) 2 red and 2 yellow counters *play or real money*	movement turns money
Rock around the clock	1	36 cards 3 sheets	20 each red and yellow counters *timer* *calculator (optional)*	time (digital, analogue) hours and half hours

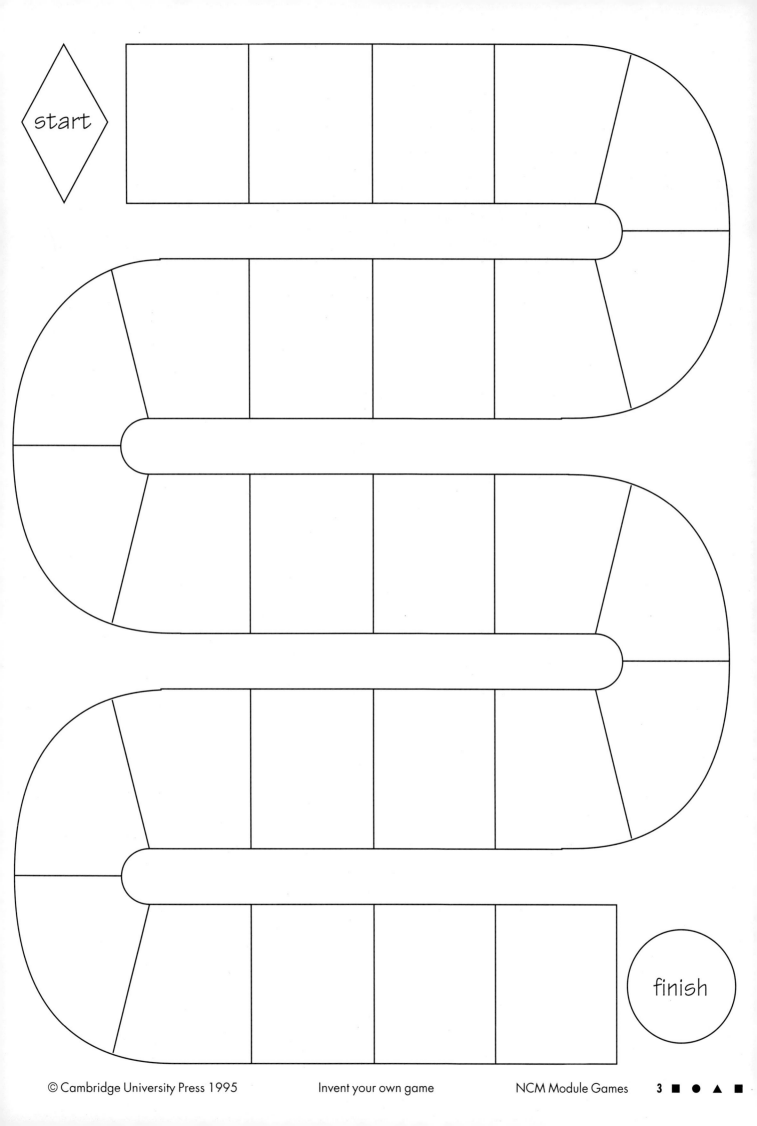

start

finish

Invent your own game   NCM Module Games   3 ■ ● ▲ ■

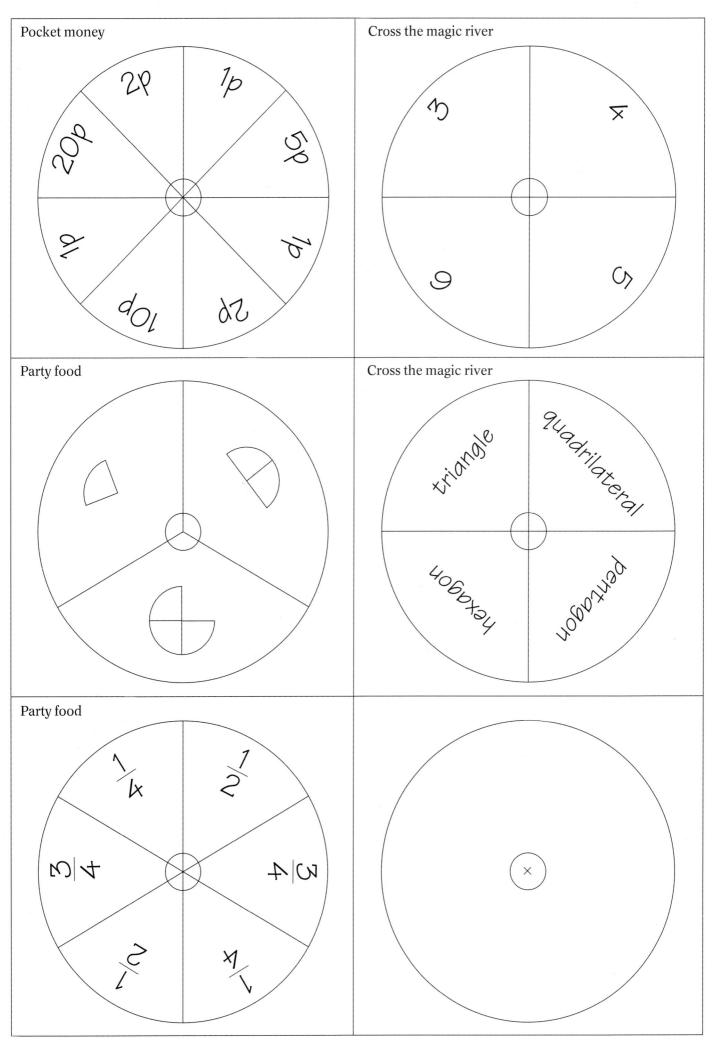

Pocket money

Cross the magic river

Party food

Cross the magic river

Party food

Stamps

Learning objectives

Sorting; addition (to 12/50); money; 2D shape

■ Game 1 Making sets

Learning objective: sorting

You need: 2 or more players
            all the cards, shuffled

Sort the cards into sets. Talk about your choices.

▲ Game 2 Dominoes

Learning objective: matching attributes (shape, colour, numeral)

You need: 2 or 4 players
            all the cards, shuffled

Deal out the cards equally. Put them face up so that they can be seen. The player with the highest value red card puts a card in the middle (or make up some other rule for starting). Take it in turns to place a card at one end of the line in the middle. There must be at least one thing in common with the adjacent card.

The winner is the first player to put down all their cards.

● Game 3 Matching

Learning objective: matching attributes (shape, colour, numeral)

This game is played like game 2, but you can make up your own rules for matching; eg adjacent cards must have two things in common; nothing in common; only one thing in common; etc.

■ Game 4 Dominoes with a difference

Learning objective: matching attributes (shape, colour, numeral)

Play this game like games 2 and 3, but cards may be placed on any free side of a matching card, not necessarily making a line. Cards which are placed adjacent to two cards must match them both.

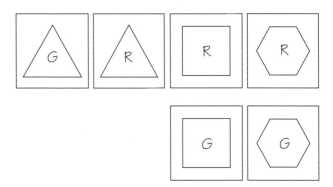

▲ Game 5

Learning objective: number of sides of 2D shapes

You need: 2 players
            a dice (1–6)
            all the cards face up randomly on the table

Take turns to throw the dice and pick up a stamp having that number of sides. If you throw a 1 that ends your go. If you throw a 2 you have another throw.

The winner is the player who collects most cards.

● Game 6

Learning objectives: number of sides of 2D shapes, matching attributes

This game is played like game 5, but the winner is the first player to collect four cards which have something in common, eg all the same colour, or shape.

■ Game 7

Learning objective: addition of numbers up to 12

You need: 2 players
2 dice (1–6)
all the cards face up randomly on the table

Take it in turns to throw both dice and add the scores. Take a card which has the price of the combined scores, if there is one.

When the stamps have all gone, the winner is the player with the most stamps.

▲ Game 8 (Extension)

Learning objective: addition to a total of 50

This is played like game 7, but the winner is the first to collect stamps to the value of 50 pence (or some other predetermined amount).

● Game 9 Stamp swap (Extension)

Learning objectives: addition, number bonds to 12

You need: 2 players
2 dice (1–6)
all the cards face up randomly on the table

This game is played like game 7, but after each turn, the player can choose to replace two or more of their cards with a card having the same total value. The swapped cards are put back on the table. The winner is the person with the least number of cards when all the cards have been picked up.

Dragon's lair

Learning objectives

Counting, addition, subtraction, developing early understandings about multiplication

■ Game 1 Dragon addition

Learning objective: addition

You need: 2–4 players
the game board
a different coloured counter for each player
orange counters for gold coins
a dice (1–6)

Put your counters on the dragon and take it in turns to throw the dice.

Move that number of spaces, say 5. Then add your dice score, 5, to the number of the space you land on, maybe a 3. 3 + 5 is 8.

Everyone does the addition to see if you can all agree, and you can check it in any way you want, such as using a number line. If you are right, you win a gold coin (counter).

The winner is the person with the most gold coins at the end of the time, or when one player has been round the board, say, twice.

▲ Game 2 Red space race

Learning objective: addition

You need: 2–4 players
the game board
a different coloured counter for each player
orange counters for gold coins
2 dice (1–6)

Take it in turns to throw both dice and add the numbers together. Move that number of spaces.

If you land on a red space, your throw the two dice again and add them together. Everyone does the addition to see if you can all agree and you can check it in any way you want. If you are right, you win two gold coins.

Each time you go past the start you win two more gold coins.

The winner is the player with the most gold coins at the end of the time.

● Game 3 (Support) Coloured spaces race

Learning objective: number recognition

You need: 2–4 players
the game board
a different coloured counter for each player
a dice (1–6)
orange counters for gold coins
one red, blue, green and yellow counter in a bag or a box so that players can't see the colours

Take it in turns to throw the dice and then also take one counter out of the bag without looking. You might throw 5 and take out the yellow counter which tells you to move to the next space that has a 5 and is yellow.

The first player to get right round to the start again wins a gold coin and another game is started.

The winner is the player with the most gold coins at the end, or you could race to be the first to get 5 gold coins.

■ Game 4 Dragon's subtraction

Learning objective: subtraction

You need: 2–4 players
the game board
a different coloured counter for each player
a dice (1–6)
50 cubes each for gold coins (Ideally these
should be made into 5 ten strips.)

Each start with 50 gold coins (cubes).

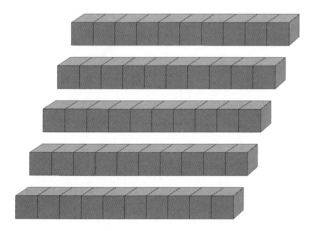

Take it in turns to throw the dice and move that
number of spaces.

You must give back to the dragon the number of
gold coins of the space you land on, say 5.

The winner is the player who gets back to the
dragon (the start) with the fewest gold coins, or
who gets rid of all their coins first on the way
round.

(You can change the game so that the winner is the
person who gets round keeping most of their
coins.)

Extension

Play game 4 but each time you give some coins
back to the dragon, you must say how many coins
you are left with, eg if you start with 50 and need to
give back 5 you might say, 'I had 50 and I gave back
5, so now I have 10, 20, 30, 40 and 5, that's 45.'

▲ Game 5 Dragon's multiplication

Learning objective: multiplication

You need: 2–4 players
the game board
a different coloured counter for each player
a dice (1–6)
orange counters for gold coins
dragon fire cards
cubes in sets of 10, 5, 3 and 2, or
Cuisenaire or Dienes rods in those bases

Sort out the dragon fire cards and play with just the
red ones.

Take it in turns to throw the dice and move that
number of spaces. Take the top card.

If you land on, say, 5 follow the instructions for 5.
So if you picked up, '4 lots of...' you must put out 4
lots of 5.

Put out 4 lots of 5 in cubes like this: (or 4 rods that
are 5 units long)

O O O O O

O O O O O

O O O O O

O O O O O

and tell the players what you have done. You might
say, 'I've put out 4 lots of 5, that's 5 and 5 and 5 and
another 5 and that makes 20 altogether.'

Hint: If the children are not good at waiting, they
can all set out the cubes or rods.

If the other players agree that you have got it right
(you could check it on the calculator if you want),
you win a gold coin. **You can't win a gold coin
unless you tell the other players what you have
done!**

The winner is the player with the most gold coins at
the end of your time.

Extensions

1 Use all the dragon fire cards.

2 You can only win if, at the end of the game, you can total up all your gold coins, put them in some kind of array and describe it to the others. So if you have 10 gold coins, you could say, 'I can put these coins into 5 lots of 2.' (Some numbers, such as 7, will only go into two arrays, 7 lots of 1, or 1 group of 7.)

3 Make some of your own dragon fire cards.

● Game 6 Golden numbers (Extension)

Learning objective: multiplication

You need: 2–4 players
the game board
a different coloured counter for each player
a dice (1–6)
golden number cards, shuffled
cubes, number line, calculator if wanted

Take a golden number card and move to the next space round the track with that number, say 10.

Now throw the dice. Multiply your score by the number you are on, so if you throw 3, that is 3 multiplied by 10. You can use anything you want to work that out. The other players should also work it out to check whether you are right.

If your answer is right, you move on 2 spaces and stay there until your next turn.

The winner is the first to get back to the dragon's lair.

■ Game 7 (Support) Golden number race

Learning objective: early multiplication

You need: 2–4 players
the game board
a different coloured counter for each player
golden number cards, shuffled
cubes, number line, calculator if wanted

Take a golden number card, say 3, and move to the next space on the track with that number on.

Now choose any number you want, say 2, and use cubes (or draw on paper) to show 3 sets of 2.

O O

O O

O O

You must tell the other players what you have done, eg 'I have made 3 sets of 2.'

▲ Game 8

Make up your own game. Maybe you could think of another way to use the colours of the spaces, eg if you land on a blue space you can win 5 more gold coins, or if you land on a green space you must double your dice throw.

Rainbow race

Learning objectives

Counting, addition, subtraction, multiplication, developing an understanding of time

■ Game 1 A pot of gold at the end of the rainbow

Learning objective: counting

You need: 2–8 players
the 2 game boards
a different coloured counter for each player
2 dice (1–6) (1 for each board)

Each player puts their counter on the rain cloud. Up to 4 players can use each board and if you have lots of players it is a good idea to have a dice for each board.

Take it in turns to throw the dice and starting on the first red space under the rain cloud, count that number along the red spaces.

Race along the red spaces, then back along the yellow, along the green and back along the blue. The winner is the first to get to the pot of gold at the end of the rainbow.

▲ Game 2 Take it away

Learning objective: subtraction

You need: 2–8 players (4 on each board)
the 2 game boards
a different coloured counter for each player
4 dice (1–6) (2 for each board)

Each choose one colour of the rainbow and put your counter on the first space of that colour. If you have 8 players it is best to have two dice for each board.

Take it in turns to throw both dice. Take one number from the other to find how many spaces to move. If you throw, say, a 4 and a 1, you work out 4 take away 1.

$$4 - 1 = 3$$

You now move your counter 3 spaces along your part of the rainbow. If you throw 2 numbers the same, eg 3 and 3, you can't move because $3 - 3 = 0$.

The winner is the first player to get to the end of their colour.

● Game 3 Rainbow race

Learning objectives: passage of time, addition

You need: at least 3 players
the 2 game boards
a counter for each player
4 dice (1–6) (2 for each board)
20 orange counters for gold coins
cubes, calculator
some kind of timer

Set a target, eg being able to throw both the dice and add the scores to get along the red track before the egg timer runs out, or move round the whole rainbow before the pendulum swings 100 times.

Players take it in turns to be the player, the person who does the timing and the checker. (You could have a player and a checker for each board.)

Throw two dice and add the numbers together. Move your counter that number of spaces along the red track. Go on doing this until you have completed the target or run out of time.

The checkers must see that this is done correctly.

The person who is timing must call out 'time' at the end of the agreed time.

If you achieve the target, win a gold coin.

The person with the most gold coins at the end of a few games is the winner.

Then you could set a different target.

■ Game 4 Rainbow target

For up to 7 players

Learning objectives: passage of time, addition

This game is played like game 3, but you can have two players co-operating to complete the target, so you could have 4 players (2 for each board), plus 2 checkers and a timer. (If you use a kitchen timer with a bell you don't need a person to be timer.)

If you achieve your target together you could challenge another pair of players to do what you did, eg if you threw the dice and moved along the whole track before the egg timer ran out, see if another pair can do that. You could keep a chart of who can reach your target.

▲ Game 5 (Extension) Rainbow multiplication

Learning objectives: multiplication and passage of time

This is played like game 3, but when you throw both dice multiply the two numbers together. You could use a calculator to help with this.

You might want to choose a difficult target for this such as moving around all the track, onto the gold, then counting along the animals and ending up at the ark in five minutes.

● Game 6 Cube race

Learning objectives: passage of time

You need: 2 or 3 players
the 2 game boards
lots of cubes (It is difficult to play this with counters.)
timer

Choose a very quick target, such as putting a blue cube on every blue space before the 10 second tocker stops. Place cubes on the spaces as quickly as possible. It doesn't matter if they get jogged a bit as you play.

You could make up your own rules for how to start, such as all the cubes must be on the desk at the start or you can let players hold them in their hands.

One or two players can try to reach the target using a board each while another player is watching the timer and is ready to tell them when to stop.

Then other players try to reach the target. The winner is the one who gets most cubes on in the time.

Now choose a different target.

■ Game 7 (Support)

Learning objectives: counting and addition

You need: 2–8 players
the 2 game boards
a counter for each player
2 dice (1–6)

Each choose a colour (or two colours each if there are not many players).

Take it in turns to throw both dice and add the scores and move along that number of spaces.

You must get the exact number to finish.

▲ Game 8 Pairs

Learning objective: pairs

You need: 2–4 players (with 4 players they need to co-operate in pairs with a board per pair)
the 2 game boards
a dice (1–6)
cubes

Take it in turns to throw the dice, and collect that number of cubes (or counters, buttons or small plastic sorting animals). With 4 players, one player from a pair throws the dice then a player from the other pair has a turn.

The player or pair must decide how many pairs they can make with their cubes, eg if 5 is thrown they can make 2 pairs and 1 left over. Use the pairs of cubes to cover pairs of animals and put any left over cubes back.

The winner is the first to cover all 10 pairs. You must throw the exact number to finish. So if you have one more pair to cover, you need to throw a 2 or a 3.

● Game 9

Make up your own game. You could try playing with a 10 sided dice, or make some cards that you take when it is your turn. These might say, 'Cover 10 red spaces.' or 'Take off any 6 of your counters.'

Jungle journey

Learning objectives

Counting, addition, choosing the shortest route, making decisions

■ Game 1

Learning objectives: addition, choosing the shortest route, making decisions

You need: 2–4 players
the game board
9 counters a different colour for each player
9 animal cards shuffled
2 dice (1–6)

Each put one of your colour counters at the start (the hexagon).

Put the cards in a pile face down, and each take one. Your card shows which animal you must visit first. You need to work out your quickest route to that animal. You can go past any of the other animals and each animal counts as one space on your journey.

Take it in turns to throw the 2 dice. Add the numbers together and move that number of spaces.

When you reach your animal, put a counter of your colour on it. Then pick another card from the pile and move towards that animal. You don't need to get an exact number to land on an animal. If you have thrown 5 and need 2 to get to your animal, you can use the other 3 to move off to the next animal.

When all the animal cards are used, collect them up, and shuffle them to make a new pile.

The winner is the player who visits the most animals in the time.

▲ Game 2 (Support)

Learning objective: counting

This game is played like game 1 but without the cards and using just one dice. Visit the animals in any order you like, leaving a counter of your colour on those visited.

The winner is the player who visits all the animals first.

● Game 3 Four animal jungle journey

Learning objectives: addition, choosing the shortest route, making decisions

For 2 or 3 players. (When there are just 2 players the game is quicker if you play with 3 dice.)

This game is played like game 1 but you draw 3 or 4 animal cards each from the pile at the start (3 cards with 3 players, 4 cards with 2 players). You then set off on your journey and visit the animals in any order you choose.

If you land on a red space you can move on 5 more spaces.

The winner is the first player to visit all their animals.

■ Game 4

Play any of the games above but use the different coloured spots for different things. Make up some rules yourself. For example, you could say that if you land on a red space you can move straight on to your next animal, or you can have another dice throw or you must go back 5 spaces.

Decide on the rules before you start. You might want to write them down so you don't forget.

You can change the game a bit by playing with a 10 sided dice, or you can do things like taking out the leopard card and saying that no player may go on the leopard, so you must find other routes to get around it.

Clown coconuts

Learning objectives

Sharing equally, mental addition, subtraction, multiplication and division; encountering prime numbers (game 6). The aim of the game is for children to develop a familiarity with multiples of numbers. For example they will gradually learn that 12 can be divided by 2, 3 and 4, but not by 5.

■ Game 1

Learning objectives: sharing equally, mental addition

You need: 2–6 players
the game board
2 dice (1–6)
brown cubes or buttons for coconuts
red cubes or buttons for the red noses
(or make some from egg boxes)
yellow cubes

Take it in turns to throw both the dice. Add the numbers together and take that number of coconuts. So if you throw 4 and 2 you take 6 coconuts.

Decide which clown has the right number of tubs for you to share your coconuts equally between them. Then share out your coconuts between the tubs.

If you can share them equally you win a red nose.

The winner is the player with the most red noses at the end.

▲ Game 2

Learning objectives: sharing equally, mental addition

This game is played like game 1, but each time you choose a clown you put a yellow cube on that clown as well as sharing out the coconuts in the tubs.

When a clown has been used 3 times (so it has 3 yellow cubes on it) it may not be used again. So, if you throw a 4, and the clowns with 2 and 4 tubs have already been used 3 times, you cannot go and must wait for your next turn.

The winner has the most red noses at the end.

Extension

(You need extra cubes, a different colour for each player.) Put a cube of your own colour on each clown when you use it. You can each use every clown only 3 times. You will need to put these coloured cubes into a tower on the clowns otherwise they will get in the way of the coconuts.

● Game 3

Learning objectives: sharing equally, mental addition, deciding on a strategy to win the largest (least) number

You need: lots of extra coconuts (buttons, cubes etc.)

This game is played like game 1 but this time you keep all the coconuts in one of the tubs each time you share coconuts, instead of winning a red nose. So if you throw 6 and share the coconuts between the 3 tubs of the green clown, you win 2 coconuts.

You can decide on your own rules for how many times you are allowed to use each clown and put a cube on the clowns as before. You might want to make each game quite short unless you have a great many coconuts available.

The winner is the player with most coconuts at the end. (Variation: the winner is the player with least coconuts at the end.)

■ Game 4 (Extension)

Learning objectives: sharing equally, mental addition, multiplication and division

You need: 2–6 players
the game board
2 dice (1–6)
brown counters for coconuts
calculator

Take it in turns to throw both dice and multiply them together to find your number of coconuts. So if you throw 6 and 4 you have 24 coconuts to share out. You might want to do your multiplication on a calculator.

At the start of the game decide whether to win a red nose or all the coconuts in one tub when you are right. (You will needs lots of brown counters if you keep the coconuts in one tub.)

You could decide to use each clown only a limited number of times.

The winner is the player with most red noses or coconuts at the end.

▲ Game 5 (Extension)

Learning objectives: sharing equally, mental addition, subtraction, multiplication and division

Play any of the above games with more than 2 dice, or with dice with more than 6 sides.

If you play with 4 dice you could choose how to use the numbers. For example, if you score 2, 4, 5 and 6, you could add them, or add some of the numbers and subtract others, eg $2 + 4 = 6$, take away $6 = 0$ add $5 = 5$. This will let you make the best numbers for the sharing.

If you combine this rule with only being allowed to use each clown 3 times, it could mean that you would not need to miss so many goes.

You need to be clear whether the winner is the player with most or least red noses or coconuts at the end.

● Game 6

Learning objectives: sharing equally, mental addition, subtraction, multiplication and division; encountering prime numbers (extension)

Make up your own game. You could make some cards saying such things as

'Divide up 100 coconuts.'
'Share out 87 coconuts.'

Are some numbers better than others to use on the cards?
Which numbers are not very good for sharing?

You could use a calculator if you put very large numbers on your cards (eg share 144 coconuts) and you might want to do the sharing on the calculator, not with lots of cubes. Or you could make some much larger tubs on pieces of paper so that you have space to share out the cubes.

Escape from the crocodile

Learning objectives

Counting, addition, number bonds, strategy

■ Game 1

Learning objectives: addition, number bonds to 12, developing simple strategy skills

You need: 2 players
the game board
2 different coloured counters for each player
2 dice (1–6)

The aim is to escape from the crocodile swamp and race to the clearing.
The yellow spaces mean 'move on 2', the red spaces mean 'go back to the start'.

Put both your counters in the swamp at the start of one of the double tracks.

Take turns to throw both dice and add their score. You can use the total in any way you like. For example, a score of 3 and 4 gives a total of 7. You could move one counter 7 spaces along one track, or move one counter 5 spaces on one track and the other counter 2 spaces on the other track. This allows you to use the 'move on 2' spaces and avoid the 'go back to the start' spaces.

The winner is the first to get both counters to the clearing, which is one step off the end of the track. You don't have to get the exact number to win.

▲ Game 2

Make your own variation on game 1, for example:

- Throw 3 dice. Subtract the value of any one from the total of the other two.

- Devise different purposes for the red and yellow spaces.

● Game 3 (Support)

Learning objective: to practise counting

This game is like game 1, but move only one counter each turn. You can decide which counter to move.

Robot Rummy

Learning objectives

Matching, sorting, identifying criteria for groups, 2D shape, counting

You need the cards for each game.

■ Game 1 Matching and sorting

For 2 or more players

Find ways to sort the cards into groups, eg all the robots with 6 buttons, or all the triangular robots.

▲ Game 2 Snap

For 2–4 players

Shuffle the cards and deal them out to all the players. You mustn't look at your cards. Place them in a pile face down in front of you.

Take it in turns to turn over a card and put it face up on a pile in the middle so that everyone can see it.

If there is some way that this card is the same as the previous one, any player can call 'snap'. They must then say what is the same, eg 'same shape', or 'same colour'.

If they are correct that player wins all the cards on the pile, and puts them at the bottom of their pile.

You can decide on the rule for snap, eg you could just snap for shape.

The winner is the player with all or most of the cards at the end.

● Game 3 Pelmanism

For 2–6 players

Spread out all the cards face down on the table.

Take it in turns to turn over two cards from anywhere on the table. Make sure that everyone can see them.

If the two cards match in some way, you can keep the pair.

Before you begin to play, you can decide on rules for matching. You could make it difficult by saying that pairs must have the same number of buttons, the same shape and must have their hands in the same position (both cards must have hands up/down.) The only thing that can be different is the colour. Or you can make it easier by allowing pairs to be the same colour or same shape.

If the cards don't match they are then turned back very carefully keeping them in the same position on the table. Players must try to remember where the cards are.

The winner is the player who ends up with the most pairs.

■ Game 4 Robot rummy

For 2–4 players

Shuffle the cards and deal out 5 to each player. Place the rest face down in the centre of the table and turn over the top card to start a second pile.

The aim is to make sets of 3 cards that go together in some way, eg 3 hexagonal robots, or 3 robots with 6 buttons or 3 robots that are the same colour.

Look at your cards and, if you want, you can put them down on the table in front of you. (The game is harder if you can hold your cards in your hands without the other players seeing them.)

Take it in turns to take a card from the centre. You can take the top one that is face up if you want it, or you can take the top one of the face down pile.

Look at the card and if you want to keep it, you must throw away one of your other cards by placing it on the face up pile.

If you can make a set of three cards that go together in some way, say 'rummy'. Place the three cards on the table where everyone can see them and say why they go together, eg 'They are all triangles with 2 buttons.' If the other players agree, then put the rummy cards in a pile face down on the table beside you. Take 3 more cards from the central face down pile so that you have 5 cards again. (When a few rummies have been made this becomes impossible and you just play on with a few cards until everyone has made all the rummies that they can.)

If you find you can make another rummy when you pick up cards after making a rummy, you must wait until your next turn to put it on the table.

The winner is the player who makes the most rummies.

▲ Game 5 Difficult robot rummy (Extension)

When you are good at robot rummy you can make harder rules for making the rummies, eg each rummy must be made up of 3 cards with the same shape robot and the buttons on the robots must add up to 12. You can try to make up some rules that no-one else has thought of.

You could also devise a scoring system for your rummies so that a complex rummy, with several attributes the same, scores much more than a rummy with just one attribute the same. For example you could score 10 points for each attribute that's the same, so if the robots are all green, have the same number of buttons and have the hands in the same position you would score 30. You will need to make a note of your score so you don't forget, and you can use a calculator to help you find the total.

● Game 6

Make up your own rules for a game. It could be a hard version of snap where you can only call snap if the shape is the same and the arms are in the same position and the button number is the same.

You might be able to make a dominoes game where one player lays down a card and the next player puts a card next to it that matches it in some way.

If you have a sorting tree of some kind (see activity 2.4 in Module 2 Teacher's resource book) you could use the cards for the sorting.

Don't block me in!

Learning objectives

Counting, odd and even numbers, making decisions, solving problems, finding the shortest route, developing strategies, developing reasoning (what if...?)

You need: 2 players
a counter each
a dice (1–6)
lots of brown cubes as bricks for the walls

The aim of the game it to get to the golden apple first. You can build walls with cubes to block your opponent's way to the treasure. You can only build on the pale green grass but your wall does not have to be continuous. Part of the wall is already built (in stone).

Put your counters on start (the red and blue circles) and take turns to throw the dice.

If the throw is an **odd number** you can **either** move 2 spaces towards the golden apple **or** put a brick on your opponent's side.
If the throw is an **even number** you can move 2 spaces **and** put a brick on the wall.
Diagonal moves are not allowed.

You can walk on the grass and on the vine to get to the golden apple but you can't build wall on the vine. So there is always a route for each player to reach the apple.

The winner is the first to reach the golden apple.

Gold diggers' island

Learning objectives

Co-ordinates; counting, addition, multiplication; use of a calculator

■ Game 1

Learning objectives: simple co-ordinates, counting to 30

You need: 2 or 3 players
the game board
all the cards, shuffled
one counter for each player
(different colours)
60 orange counters for gold coins
1 dice (1–6) and calculator
(for games 3 and 4)

Place the cards in a pile face down.

Players take it in turns to look at the top card and move their counter to that square. If it is a square with treasure, take that many gold coins (orange counters). Put the used cards to one side. If players put their counter on the wrong square, they must replace the card at the bottom of the pile, and miss that turn.

The winner is the player with most gold coins when all the cards have been used.

▲ Game 2

Learning objectives: simple co-ordinates, counting to 30, early subtraction

This game is played like game 1, but if you land on a pirate you loose 2 gold coins, and if you land on a magic fish you have another turn.

● Game 3 (extension)

Learning objectives: simple co-ordinates, addition, using a calculator

This game is played like game 2, but when you land on a treasure square, throw the dice and add the dice score to the number in the square to find the number of gold coins you win. Keep a record of your scores. Add up your total carefully using a calculator.

■ Game 4 (further extension)

Learning objectives: simple co-ordinates, multiplication, using a calculator

This game is played like game 2, but when you land on a treasure square, throw the dice and multiply the dice score with the number in the square to find the number of gold coins you win. Keep a record of your scores. Add up your total carefully using a calculator.

Pocket money

Learning objectives

Money (to £1), giving change, days of the week

■ Game 1

Learning objectives: using money up to £1, exchanging coins, giving change, addition of money; names and order of the days of the week

You need: 2 to 4 players
the game board
a different coloured counter each
1 dice (1–6)
play money in a tray

Each time you pass over a blue Saturday space, collect 10p.
You also collect money when you land on green spaces.
When you land on red spaces you spend money. You can take change from the tray in any way you like.

Put your counters on the starting Monday.

Each player starts with 30p. Some ways of making 30p are shown in the middle of the board.

Take turns to throw the dice, and move that number of spaces round the board, collecting and spending money.

The winner has most money after a set time.

▲ Game 2

Learning objectives: using money up to £1, exchanging coins, giving change, addition of money, doubling numbers; names and order of the days of the week

This game is played like game 1, but you have 50p to start with, and when you land on a red square you buy 2 of each item, one for you and one for a friend.

● Game 3 (Extension)

Learning objectives: money up to £1, exchanging coins, giving change, addition of money, multiplication; names and order of the days of the week

This game is played like game 1, but multiply the sum of money by your dice score to find out how much you spend or collect.

Palm tree pennies

Learning objectives

Money to 20p, recognition of coins, exchange of coins

■ Game 1 Matching pictures of coins

Learning objective: recognising coins to 20p

You need: 1 player
1 game board
selection of coins, preferably real

Cover the values on the picture with the correct coins.

▲ Game 2 Matching coins to value

Learning objective: recognising coins to 20p

You need: 2 players
2 boards
spinner for 1p 1p 1p 2p 2p 5p 10p 20p
selection of coins for a 'bank'

Take turns to spin the spinner. Take the coin of that value and place it on your board. If all available spaces of that value are covered already, you cannot go.

The winner is the first to cover all the coin spaces on their game board.

● Game 3 Exchanging to 20p

Learning objectives: exchanging coins to 20p

You need: 2 players
2 game boards
selection of coins including at least twenty 1p pieces
1 dice (1–6)

Take turns to throw the dice and take that number of 1 pence coins from the 'bank'. These can be placed on the trunk of the palm tree.

When you have enough 1p coins you can exchange them for a coin of higher value to put on the board.

The winner is the first to cover all the coin spaces on their board.

■ Game 4 Exchanging to 20p

Learning objectives: exchanging coins to 20p

You need: 2 players
2 game boards
spinner for 1p 1p 1p 2p 2p 5p 10p 20p
selection of coins

This is played like game 2 but players take the coin shown on the spinner each time they spin. They can then exchange coins for others of the same total face value in order to cover the board, eg 5 pennies for one 5p coin or one 20p coin for 10p and two 5p coins.

▲ Game 5 Matching coins to value

Learning objectives: recognising coins to 20p

You need: 2 players
2 game boards
selection of coins
spinner for 1p 1p 1p 2p 2p 5p 10p 20p

Cover the boards with the correct coins. Take turns
to spin the spinner and remove the appropriate
coin. If there is no coin left of that value you cannot
remove a coin, and must wait for your next turn.
The winner is the first to clear their board.

● Game 6 Exchanging to 20p

Learning objective: exchanging coins to 20p

You need: 2 players
2 game boards
selection of coins
a dice (1–6)

Cover the boards with the correct coins. Take turns
to throw the dice, and remove that many 1 pence
pieces from the trunk of the tree. Before each
subsequent throw, you can 'refill' the trunk by
exchanging some of the higher value coins on your
board for 1 pence pieces from the bank. Any
surplus coins that will not fit on the trunk can be
placed on the parrots. The winner is the first to
clear their board.

■ Game 7

Make up your own game.

Cross the magic river

Learning objectives

2D shape, strategy

■ Game 1

Learning objectives: recognition of 2D shapes (triangle, quadrilateral, pentagon and hexagon); strategy and planning skills.

You need: 2 players
the game board
12 red, 12 yellow counters
6 animal cards
spinner for 3, 4, 5, 6

Place three animal cards on each cart at the top of the board.

One player uses the red counters, the other player uses the yellow counters.

Take turns to spin the spinner. Place one of your counters in a shape in the first row with that number of sides. If there isn't one you miss a go. All following times you spin, the shape you use must be touching a shape you have already covered. It can touch just at the corners. You may not place a counter in a space that is already occupied.

The first to create a path across the river takes one of the animals across, and puts an animal card in their coloured cart. Clear the board and start again.

The winner is the first player to bring all three animals across the river.

▲ Game 2

Learning objectives: recognition of 2D shapes (triangle, quadrilateral, pentagon and hexagon); strategy and planning skills.

This game is played like game 1 but all the animal cards are laid in a row across the top of the board. Players can move any of the animals across. The winner is the player to have brought the most animals across the river in a given time.

● Game 3

Learning objectives: recognition of 2D shapes (triangle, quadrilateral, pentagon and hexagon), familiarity with shape names; strategy and planning skills.

This game is played like game 1 but use a spinner with the names of the shapes: triangle, quadrilateral, pentagon, hexagon, instead of the number of sides.

Party food

Learning objectives

Recognition of half, quarter, three quarters, whole, in picture and (extension) numerals; equivalence of half and two quarters; addition to 16.

■ Game 1

Learning objectives: strategy, addition to 16

You need: 2 players
the 2 boards (one for each player)
all the cards spread out and placed face down.

Take turns to pick a card. Place the card anywhere on a plate on your board. The second and subsequent cards chosen can be placed next to other chosen cards to make a cake, or used to start a new cake.

The winner is the player who has the cake with the most candles.

▲ Game 2

Learning objectives: understanding halves

You need: 2 players
2 boards
all the cards, shuffled and placed in a pile, face down

Take turns to take a card from the top of the pile, and place it on the game board. The aim is to cover half of each plate. The pieces of cake on a plate must have the same number of candles. Cards which cannot be used are placed on a new pile and re-used when the first pile is finished.

The winner is the first to cover **half** of each plate.

● Game 3

Learning objectives: language and equivalence of half, quarter, three quarters

You need: 2 players
game boards and cards
spinner with fraction pictures

Shuffle the cards and put them in a pile, face down.

Take turns to spin the spinner and say aloud what it shows: 'This is one quarter so I'm going to take a quarter of a cake. I need one card.' The player takes the correct number of cards from the top of the pile and arranges them on a plate on the game board.

The winner is the first to cover all their plates.

■ Game 4

Learning objectives: half, quarter, three quarters; strategy

This is played like game 3, but this time each cake must have the same number of candles on each quarter. Cards which cannot be used are placed face down on a new pile and then re-used when the first pile is finished.

▲ Game 5

Learning objectives: fractions and addition to 10

This is played like game 3, except that the candles on each cake must add up to 10. The winner is the player with the most complete cakes with 10 candles.

● Game 6 (Extension)

Learning objective: recognition of fraction numerals

You need: 2 players
the game boards and cards
spinner with fraction numerals

Play game 3 using the fraction numeral spinner.
Say aloud what the spinner shows, and the number
of cards to be taken. 'This shows a half, so I'm
going to take half a cake. I need to take two cards.'
Games 4 and 5 can also be played using the
numeral spinner instead of the spinner with
fraction pictures.

Turtle money trail

Learning objectives

Movement (translation and rotation), money to 50p, number bonds.

Before you begin

On the direction cards, 'Forward 1' means one step in the direction that the turtle counter is facing. 'Left 1' means turn 1 right-angle to the turtle's left. You may need to remind children that they stay on the same square when they turn.

Children may find it helps to move round the board to face the same direction as their turtle when working out how to make the turn.

■ Game 1

Learning objectives: use of translational (forward and back) and rotational (turning) movement; counting with 1p, 2p, 5p and 10p coins

You need: 2 players
the game board
32 direction cards, shuffled
2 turtles
1p, 2p, 5p and 10p coins

Each place your turtle on one of the red starfish, with the turtle facing in any direction you choose.

Put the cards in a pile face down. Take it in turns to take the top card and move your turtle according to the directions given on the card.

If the turtle lands on a coin square, collect that amount of money from the bank. If the turtle moves off the board, put it back on a red starfish facing in any direction, and collect 1p.

The first player to collect 20p wins. Alternatively, the player with most money after a set time wins.

▲ Game 2

Learning objectives: use of translational (forward and back) and rotational (turning) movement; counting with 1p, 2p, 5p and 10p coins; doubling numbers

This game is played like game 1 but if you land on a coin square throw a dice. An even throw means double your takings from the bank.

● Game 3

Learning objectives: use of translational (forward and back) and rotational (turning) movement; counting with 1p, 2p, 5p and 10p coins; simple subtraction

This game is played like game 1 but if you land on a magic fish you win 10p. If you land on a sea shell you lose 2p. The first to collect 50p wins.

■ Game 4

Learning objectives: addition and counting with 1p, 2p, 5p and 10p coins; number bonds and strategy skills

You need: 2 players
the game board
dice (1–6)
2 red and 2 yellow counters

Decide who will use the red and who the yellow counters. Place the red counters at the bottom of columns 1 and 2, the yellow counters at the bottom of columns 7 and 8.

Take turns to throw the dice. Split the score between your two counters, and move them up. The object is to move them to gain the most money.

When both players reach the opposite end of the board, the winner is the one with most money.

Rock around the clock

■ Game 1

Learning objectives: recognising time in hours and half hours on analogue and digital clock faces, understanding the passage of time, addition of minutes.

You need: 2 players
the game board
20 red and 20 yellow counters
the two sets of cards shuffled separately
some kind of timer for game 3 (a kitchen timer is ideal)
a calculator if you wish

Decide who will use the red and who the yellow counters.

Shuffle the white cards and place them face down in the middle. Take it in turns to take a white card. Tell your partner what it says.

Place one of your counters on a clock that says that time and discard the card. You cannot put a counter on a clock that is already covered. You are more likely to win the game if you can find a clock in the middle picture that shows the time.

When you put a counter on one of the clocks in the middle, take the top yellow card from the pile.

When all the white cards have been used, shuffle them and re-use them.

When all the clocks are covered count up all the time on your yellow cards. The player with the most time wins.

▲ Game 2 (Support)

Learning objective: recognising hours and half hours on clocks

This game is similar to game 1, but you don't use the yellow cards. The player with most counters on the board wins.

● Game 3 Ten minute race

Learning objective: understanding the passage of time

This game is played like game 1 or game 2. Set a timer of some kind to show when 10 minutes is up, or get someone to time you with a stop watch.

The player with most counters on the board, or most time on their yellow cards after 10 minutes wins.

Introduction to the mats

Philosophy and aims

The mats are designed to provide a stimulating resource for young children which may be used in a variety of ways to develop their mathematical understanding and to provide opportunities for the development of practical work and discussion. They can be used very flexibly to support various teaching styles and abilities of children.

The mats provide practice and reinforcement on all areas of the mathematics curriculum. Each mat has been designed with a particular mathematical concept in mind, but many have more than one concept featured. This allows you, the teacher, to select what appeals to you and your children. Each mat has a clearly defined border depicting a particular feature or concept, many of which can be used for playing games or carrying out simple investigations.

The mats can also be used for assessment and review. The Teacher's resource book gives detailed advice on how some of the mats can be used in this way, but many of the others can be used equally as well.

The main emphasis in this pack is on activities which are suitable for use with five or six year old children, but suggestions are also included for further development work and extension activities to show how they can be used with a wider age range if so desired.

One copy of each mat is available in this pack. It is often useful to have further copies so several children can work on the same one at once. The Extra mats pack enables you to buy as many extra copies as you wish.

How to use this book

Within this book there is a section on each mat. These outline some of the key concepts which could be introduced using the mats and list the suggested resources which may be used for practical work. Restrictions on space mean that we can only give a summary of possible activities. The sections below give some ideas on how these can be expanded to suit your children and ways of working. Some mats have sample resource sheets which can be photocopied for recording and follow-up tasks.

How to use the mats

The same principles may be applied to any of the mats and these are outlined below. It is important always to start with discussion and this can lead to practical activities, investigations and problem solving, simple games, assessment and review, and recording.

Discussion

Discussion is the most important aspect of the work. It is very important throughout to give the children plenty of time to think and respond to questions. Ask questions of each member of the group to ensure that all children take part in the discussion.

Start by asking open-ended questions such as,

> 'What can you see on this mat?'
> 'What shapes can you find?'
> 'What do you like about this mat?'

After this initial observation of the mat, the questions can focus on more specific areas. For example, with the Calendar mat, you could ask questions such as,

> 'What can you tell me about the summer?'
> 'What was the weather like in February?'
> 'What is the weather like today?'

Follow up responses with further questions to focus upon detail, for example,

> 'Which plate (on the Party time mat) contains the most items?'
> 'Which cards (on the Playing cards mat) have more than 5 diamonds?'

Practical activities

Each mat is designed to stimulate a range of practical activities. Many ideas are outlined in the notes for each mat, but here are some general activities which can be applied to most mats.

- ■ 'Point to the ....'

- ▲ Matching and sorting using appropriate comparisons.

- ● Counting using counters or objects. Making comparisons.

- ▦ Measuring using string, ribbon, etc. Making comparisons.

As part of the reinforcement process, it is a good idea to follow the practical activities with some form of recording.

The following ideas make use of the lamination of the mats.

- ▦ Use clay or plasticine to produce 'blobs' to press onto the different numbers of diamonds, hearts, clubs and spades on the cards on the Playing cards mat, to help with counting.

- ▲ Make small clay, plasticine or dough vehicles or people to use as markers to move around the Town map mat. These will stay in place, while counters might slide about.

- ● Use plasticine blobs for heads of people in the boats and carriages on the Theme park mat for counting.

- ■ Use plasticine or clay and circle cutters to make shapes identical to those on the Circles mat or to make larger and smaller circles for cutting and ordering.

- ▲ Make shapes and cut them into halves and quarters to support work with the Squares and circles mat.

- ● Use plasticine to make starfish like those on the Starfish mat and press in the patterns with a pencil or other suitable object. Counting and matching can be assessed and reinforced using this method.

- ■ Press plasticine over numbers on the Hundred square mat to cover them semi-permanently, before you show it to the children. This works much better than counters which tend to move around.

Recording

Children need to be introduced to the idea of recording, but it may actually be done by the teacher or an adult helper after discussion with the child. The advantages of this are that children

- ■ begin to experience different ways of recording and can compare them,

- ▲ are encouraged to consider what the key points are that need to be recorded,

- ● begin to see the value of recording as a record and reference for further work and as a means of communication,

- ■ begin to see a logical approach to organisation of recording,

- ▲ are encouraged to record when they are ready and not before, so children's growing confidence is not harmed.

Children can record their ideas using a wide range of media. Often the only recording valued is pencil and paper and this is unfortunate as it gives a very narrow impression of how we learn and communicate mathematics. It is possible to record on the mats themselves by using a spirit pen. The recording could also be drawing, colouring, matching, filling gaps on mats resource sheets, painting, printing and model making. These may require some adult supervision. Sewing and cooking are also very worthwhile, but require a higher level of adult supervision from parent helpers or ancillary staff.

Stimulating investigation and problem solving

The mats are carefully designed to provide opportunities for open-ended investigation and a stimulus for problem solving. Some ideas are included in the notes for each mat, but there are some general features to look for when preparing work that may be applied more generally.

The introduction of free and structured investigation of mathematics at an early age helps children to develop a broad insight into the fact that there are often many ways of solving a problem. It is important to encourage children to develop confidence in exploring a variety of approaches to problem solving and to develop strategies for investigation.

Simple games

Each mat has a border some of which provide opportunities for developing games. Some ideas are provided in the notes, but you can also make up your own. These may be played by children in groups of up to four or as a teacher-directed whole-group activity. Children should also be encouraged to develop their own games using the mats and equipment such as counters and dice.

It is important to discuss with children the basic principles of playing games. These are the rules (especially start and finish rules, missing turns, extra turns, time limits set, frequency and order of play), aims (how the game will be won), and scoring (this should be kept simple, a calculator may be useful).

Assessment and review

A particularly valuable feature of the mats is that they may be used to monitor progress using practical activities, especially if several copies of each mat are available. The Teacher's resource book includes review activities based on the Playing cards, Theme park and Town map mats. However it is anticipated that any teacher using the mats will be making continuous assessments of the children as they carry out activities, and further work will be based on these assessments. It is important to give children time to consolidate their understanding of concepts before moving on to higher-level skills.

Classroom practice

It is recommended that mats are used daily in ten-minute sessions. However even five minutes' discussion can provide a wealth of mathematical ideas and vocabulary, and some children may be able to concentrate for 15 or 20 minutes while exploring an investigation together. It is expected that each mat will be used several times with each group and that on each occasion a particular aspect of the mat is used as the focus. An example of how this can be done is given on page 32.

Mats can be used with the whole class, groups, pairs and individuals. They should also be freely available for children during free choice or informal activity sessions as they can stimulate imaginative play and discussion.

Whole class use

Mats can be attached to an easel and used for general class discussion or displayed as a poster on the wall for reference. They can be useful as a general introduction to an appropriate theme or topic, for example the Calendar mat is ideal for introducing aspects of time, months and seasons as well as weather, the Starfish mat for a theme on the sea or water, the Circles and Squares and circles mats will be useful when focusing upon shape work.

Group work

Groups of up to eight children could work on a single mat around a table with the teacher or ancillary. Ideally have several copies of the same mat available so children can work in pairs or individually on the practical activities. This enables all children to be actively involved and makes assessment easier.

Paired activity

Children can be set to work together on a mat as an introduction to an activity or game or as a reinforcement for other work.

Individual work

Mats can be used to teach a new concept to an individual child or to provide an activity for a more or less able pupil. They can also be used for reinforcement for an individual child.

An example of daily 15-20 minute sessions using the School fete mat.

Session 1 General observation and discussion of all aspects of the mat.

Session 2 Introducing and recognising two-digit numbers. Use this mat in conjunction with the 100 square mat.

Session 3 Pick a number. Repeat this session several times. With a group of 10 children each child could choose or be allocated a different number to explore. The number could be one of the ticket numbers or the number of sweets in the bottles: 12, 15, ... 19, 64. Find out as much as you can about the number as in the example of 56 on page 71.

Session 4 Order the border numbers, lowest to highest. Generate some other numbers using tombola tickets taken out of a box. Start by ordering 3 numbers, then 4, and so on.

Session 5 Use the border numbers for addition; choose pairs of numbers to total. 80 + 19 = 99 43 + 50 = 93.

Session 6 Use the tombola numbers to talk about numbers ending with 0 or 5. Find these on a 100 square. Explore and order the numbers.

Session 7 Talk about numbers 'nearest to' to introduce rounding. Which number is nearest to 25? 50? Which numbers are greater/less than, say, 50?

Session 8 Use the border numbers for subtraction. Find the difference between pairs of numbers. Use a calculator to help with this. 56 – 50 = 6 43 – 33 = 10

Session 9 Talk about the people. Play the guess who game before sorting and ordering them. Extend vocabulary of description and focus upon detail as suggested in Teacher's notes.

Session 10 Using the clown game, investigate totals scored using 2 beanbags. 8 + 4, 7 + 3, 2 + 2, etc.

Extension activities for more able children

■ Investigate totals using 3 beanbags in the clown game. Start by assuming you are expert and score with all 3 bags, then consider possible scores if you miss with some.

▲ These are the totals of four players who each used 4 beanbags. How might they have scored these totals?

Jane 24 Olga 27 Peter 25 Amit 28.

What is the least number of bags needed to win each total?

■ Round numbers to the nearest multiple of 5. Use the hundred square to help with this. First use the number on the tickets then choose some of your own.

▲ Introduce the triangle number pattern using the tower of tin cans.

● Set challenges in combining the border numbers to develop estimation. For example, find 3 numbers that give a total as near to 100 as possible. Use a calculator.

Grouping children according to ability

It is possible to adapt activities so that they are suitable for different abilities. The following example shows how the Party time mat can be used with three groups of 6–8 children grouped according to mathematical ability. It is unlikely to be this simple with young children, but the example shows how a range of questions can cater for a wide ability range. Similar activities could be done on this mat based on number and multiples.

Lower ability group	Average group	More able group

Focus on 6
Look for sets of 6 on the mat, for example a plate with 6 biscuits, a cake with 6 candles, 6 ice creams. Practical tasks should follow lots of discussion about 6.
■ Use plasticine to make 6 candles for the cake on your mat.
▲ Cover the ice creams with 6 counters.
● Write the number 6 six times
■ Draw sets of 6 objects:
    6 biscuits
    6 ices
    6 of anything you like
	Explore 9
	Talk about the shape of the plates. Which has 9 items on it? Consider the different items on the mat and discuss how many more of each item you would need to make 9. For example:
	There are 6 ices, so 3 more are needed;
	There are 4 lollies so 5 more are needed.
	
	Focus on the 9 biscuits. Consider the patterns: 3 lots of 3.
	
	Lay out 9 cubes to make a 3 by 3 pattern. Discuss this special pattern.
	
	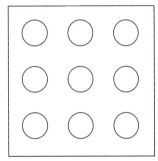
	
	Draw a set of 3 lots of 3.
	■ Investigate other square plates having 4 lots of 4, 5 lots of 5, etc.
		Encourage children to describe each plate as accurately as possible using a wide vocabulary: shape of plate, type of items on each plate, number of items on each plate, sets of items on each plate. They could find plates with more or fewer items than other plates. Can they identify relationships between plates and items, for example by comparing the sizes of all the circular plates.
		
		Record all the observations.
		Introduce problem solving challenges to stimulate subtraction. For example, consider the total number of items on each plate. Then ask the children to close their eyes while you cover some of the items on the plates (to suggest they have been eaten) with large round counters. Then ask children to tell you quickly how many items are remaining on each plate.
		
		Use the large plates with several items.
		
		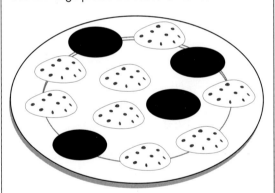
		
		12 to start with, 4 covered, 12 – 4 = 8
		Watch to see if anyone counts or some subtract. They may count in blocks, 2s or 4s. Encourage the children to tell you how they did the calculation.

Some assessment activities using the Money mat

Use a collection of real money. Ask children to:

■ Place 1 of each coin in the 7 columns indicated.

▲ Put six pennies in the 1p column.
   Put four 2ps in the 2p column.
   Put two 5ps in the 5p column.
   Put 30p in the 10p column.
   What coin goes in the fifth column? Find one.
   What coin goes in the next column?

● Can you collect 30p and sort the coins onto the mat?

■ Choose 3 values in the border, say, 53p, 11p and 27p.

Put a pile of money to total each amount on top of each value. Use as few coins as possible.

$50p + 2p + 1p \rightarrow 53p$

$10p + 1p \rightarrow 11p$

$20p + 5p + 2p \rightarrow 27p$

▲ Cover all the values greater than 60p with a counter.

● Concentrate on, say, just the lower border.

					reduced range			
£1	57p	24p	40p	75p	30p	11p	52p	10p

Read the values. Which is the greatest amount? the least? (Reduce the range for less able children.)

Cover the values in order with counters, starting with the least.

   10p, 11p, 24p, 30p, 40p, 52p, 57p, 75p, £1

For any assessment task it is important to build up to a level suitable to the ability of the child to try to encourage increased success rather than immediate failure.

Squares and circles

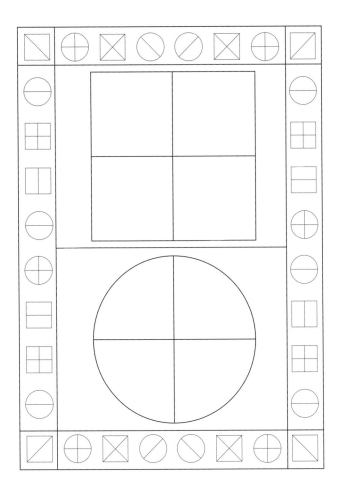

Useful resources

Counters, cubes, Squares and circles resource sheet; squares and circles of felt in at least two colours, cut to fit the centre shapes.

Teacher's notes

The large square and circle are intended to stimulate work on halves and quarters of the shapes, as well as providing a framework for partitioning sets into halves and quarters.

Using the centre

■ **Exploring patterns**. Children can explore pattern and shape using pieces of felt cut to size in halves and quarters which they arrange in different combinations on the centre shapes.

▲ **Recording patterns**. Children can record their patterns by colouring in shapes on the resource sheet. For example, using red and yellow quarter pieces they could find:

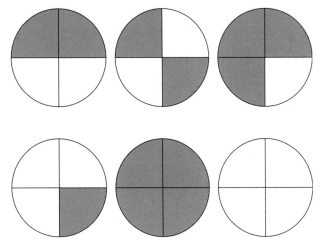

Mathematical concepts

Shape (sorting and matching squares and circles), introduction to fractions (simple halves and quarters), counting, comparison, multiplication and division, pattern.

Description of the mat

The central section is partitioned into 2 halves. One contains a large square cut into 4 equal sized small squares and the other contains a circle cut into 4 equal segments.

The border is decorated with squares and circles, divided into halves or quarters and coloured with pairs of the 6 colours: red, yellow, blue, green, orange, purple.

- **Notation**. You could introduce the notation of $\frac{1}{2}$ and $\frac{1}{4}$ and talk about 1 whole split into 4 pieces, which we write as $\frac{1}{4}$.

  This could lead to further recording:

  $\frac{1}{4}$ red $+ \frac{1}{4}$ yellow $+ \frac{1}{4}$ red $+ \frac{1}{4}$ yellow

  which could lead to the idea of recording 2 quarters as $\frac{2}{4}$. By arranging two quarters together, children may see that $\frac{2}{4} = \frac{1}{2}$. They will need lots of practical manipulation on the mat to understand this.

- ■ **Simple multiplication**. You can cover a shape with 2 halves of felt to focus on doubling or use the quarters for multiplying by 4.
  Place the same number of counter or cubes in each of the sections and find the total:

  $1 + 1 = 2$ $1 + 1 + 1 + 1 = 4$
  $2 + 2 = 4$ $2 + 2 + 2 + 2 = 8$

  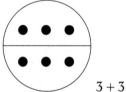

  $3 + 3 = 6$

- ▲ **Simple division**. Once children become familiar with the numbers that are multiples of 2 and 4, they can start to think about division. It is helpful to work with groups of 4 or 8 children so that they can relate the activities to the group. For example, 4 children want to share a set of counters equally. Investigate and find which numbers will share equally.

  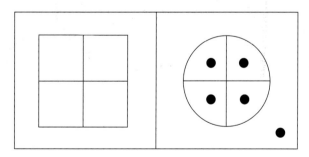

  4 counters can be shared equally. With 5 counters there is one left over.

  Let the children explore this and talk about the numbers they discover. Ask questions like 'Can 13 be shared equally?', 'What about 16?'

The logical approach is to put the same number in each of the 4 quarters. Don't tell them this – let them discover it.

This activity could make a good assessment for problem solving and logic, as well as understanding of large numbers.

- ● **Four equal sets!: a game for 2 to 4 players.** You need a dice (1–6) and counters. Each player uses either a centre square or circle, or a copy of one. The aim of the game is to reinforce the idea of equal shares and collecting sets. Play involves addition and subtraction, problem solving and logic.

  Start by agreeing a number that is a multiple of 4 (12, 16, 20, 24, 28, …), say 24. The players take turns to roll the dice and collect the appropriate number of counters. If they have enough to put the same number in each part of the grid, they share them out, and keep any left over to put with the counters they win next go

  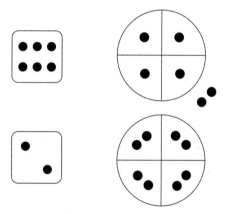

  Jan rolls 6. She places 4, keeps 2.
  Next turn she rolls 2, so now has 4.

  Play continues until one player has put 24 counters in their grid, 6 in each section.

- ■ **Other numbers.** If you have other shapes available children can be encouraged to think about multiplying and dividing into different numbers of sets.

  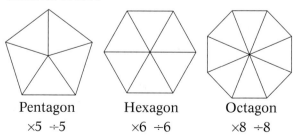

  Pentagon   Hexagon   Octagon
  ×5 ÷5   ×6 ÷6   ×8 ÷8

Using the border

■ **Counting using cubes.** Recognition of circles and squares can be revised by placing two colours of cubes or counters over the circles and squares in the border. Count and compare the sets of shapes. For example:

- Cover the circles. How many are there? (16)
- How many circles are coloured half red, half yellow, etc? (4)
- Cover the squares. How many are there? (16)
- Cover the squares that are half red and half green etc. (2)
- Find a shape that is half orange and half yellow. What is it? (circle or square)
- Can you find any shapes that are coloured identically? (2 circles, quartered and coloured red and blue, another 2 coloured red and yellow; 2 circles halved, one pair yellow and green, one pair blue and green, one pair blue and red, one pair red and yellow.)
- Are there more or less circles in any part of the border, for example the left border or top border? (same number)
- Can you find circles that are half blue? How many can you find? (six including two with 2 quarters blue.)

▲ **Discussing fractions.** The border is designed to encourage discussion of halves and quarters. Suggest that children record all the possible combinations of colours on a shape. Begin with simple halves, and record on the resource sheet. For example,

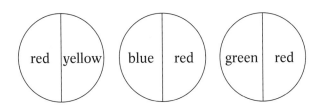

- How many combinations could there be? (30)
- How many can you find on this mat? (6)
- Which possibilities are not shown on the mat?

To simplify this reduce the numbers of colours available.

Investigating quarters would be best done using only two colours to begin with. Recording the possibilities may be appropriate and can be done on the photocopiable resource sheet. This is similar to earlier work using the centre of the mat, but children could be encouraged to be more systematic.

It is important to introduce the idea of rotation of each shape resulting in the same combination but different position.

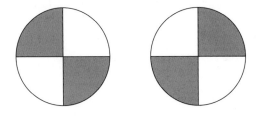

The second of these two shapes is the first turned through a $\frac{1}{4}$ turn and would count as the same design.

● **Match the colours: a game for 2 players.** You need two 6-sided dice coloured on each face with one of the six colours used in the border, 12 counters for each player (of different colours). This game challenges the children's observational skills and memory.

Take it in turns to roll the two dice. Look at the colours, for example red and yellow. Place one of your counters on a shape that is half red and half yellow. If there is no shape in the colours (for example yellow/yellow) miss a go. Play continues until one player has put down all 12 counters.

Squares and circles

Name...

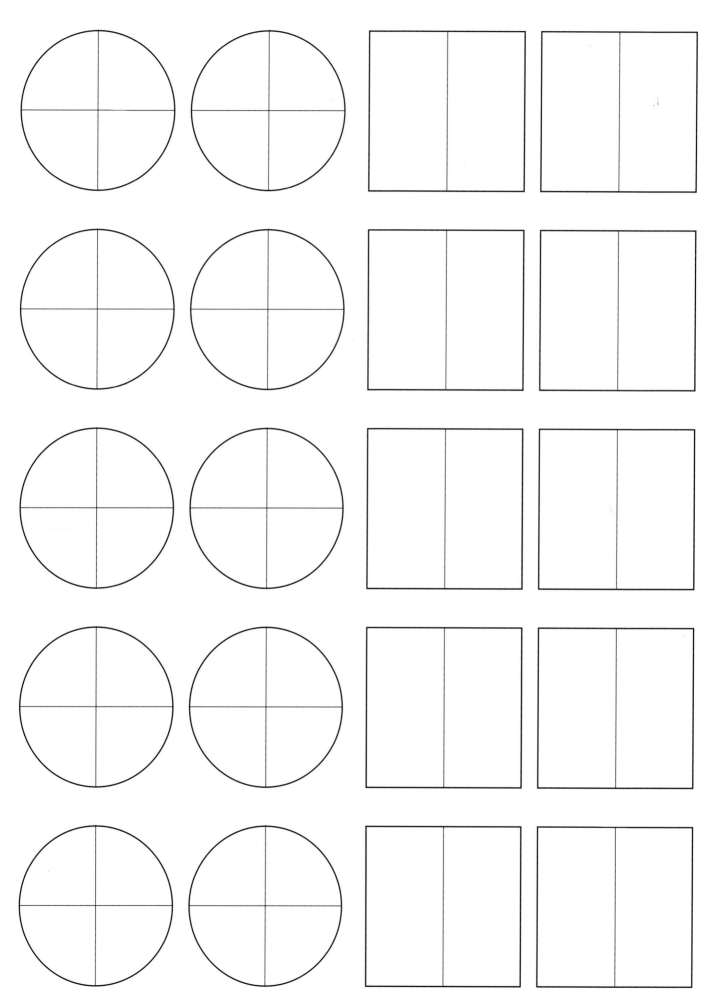

Party time

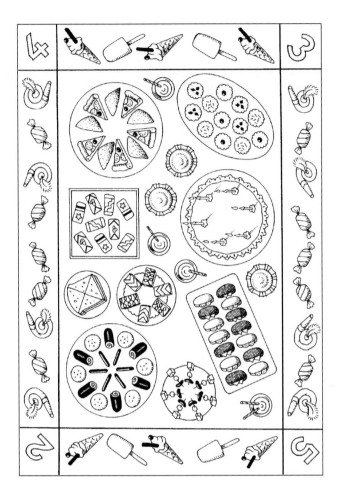

The square plate has 9 wrapped biscuits, 3 each of 3 types.

The small round plate with doiley has 6 rectangular cakes 3 each of 2 types.

The other small round plate has cheese, onion and gherkin on 7 sticks, ie 7×3 items.

There are two large round plates: one with cakes and biscuits (3×6), the other with pizza and samosas (2×5).

The long rectangular plate has 14 rolls: 7 white rolls, 7 brown rolls (2×7 or 7×2).

The very small sandwich plate is intended to provide an opportunity to begin discussion work on cutting up into fractions.

Three different flavoured jellys are shown, four drinks, and a birthday cake with 6 candles.

The border shows party items (4 ice lollies, 6 ice creams, 8 blowers and 10 sweets) for matching and sorting activities, with numbers 2 to 5 in the corners.

Mathematical concepts

Number, addition, subtraction, introduction to multiplication; matching, sorting, ordering and pattern; similarity and difference, size, shape; investigation and problem solving; data handling; money.

Description of the mat

The middle shows a collection of party food arranged on plates of various shapes, sizes and colours. Examine each plate in turn and discuss the items. There are different multiples of items arranged in patterns.

The green oval plate has 12 fancy cakes, 4 with a single cherry, 4 with three jelly diamonds, 4 with eight candy sticks.

Useful resources

Plates (paper and permanent), biscuits, cakes, sweets, etc, or items to represent food; cubes, counters, beads and laces.

Teacher's notes

■ **General discussion.** Explore the various features of the mat. Begin with the corners to reinforce number recognition. Follow this by looking at the borders, the two short sides then the top and bottom. Count and compare the numbers and colours of items. Explore 'more than', 'less than'. There is lots to look at and talk about in the middle of the mat. It is important to encourage open discussion: gather information about the children's own favourite foods, and let them choose what they would like to eat.

Focus attention on the number of items on each plate, how many of each type and general observation.

Refer to particular plates by size, shape and colour. Ask questions like 'If I eat two biscuits from the square plate, how many will be left?' Follow up focus on this plate by having 9 wrapped biscuits to share, sort and play with.

Activities using the plates

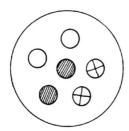

- ■ **Making plates and cakes.** Use coloured paper, scissors and crayons to make up a plate of cakes. For example, ask children to make six cakes on their plates. Once these are made encourage each child to talk about their own plate of cakes (biscuits, pizza, or whatever).

- ▲ **Making real cakes.** Make some actual cakes in class, decorate them then sit the children in groups to share them out and eat them. Count as the cakes are removed. Discuss the size and shape of the items.

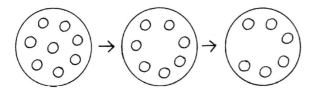

How many have been taken so far? How many are left?

Alternatively make dough cakes to play with over and over again.

Food on sticks is fun to make using plasticine or dough. Roll balls for onions, mould cubes for cheese, and sausage shapes for gherkins. Cocktail sticks may be used under supervision.

- ● **Using a class shop.** The home corner could become a shop for children to buy party food to match the items on the mat.

Send children to buy items, eg

'Jane, you go and buy the chocolate rolls.' (6)
'Josh, you go and buy the wrapped biscuits.' (9)
Money may be introduced to broaden this activity.

- ■ **Making patterns.** Give children the freedom to use counters, cubes, and other shapes to produce paper plates laid with food in patterns.

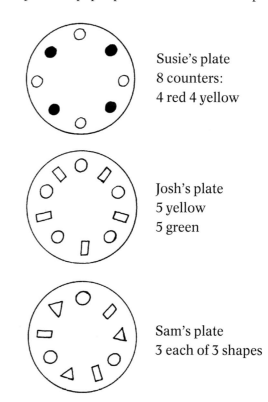

Susie's plate
8 counters:
4 red 4 yellow

Josh's plate
5 yellow
5 green

Sam's plate
3 each of 3 shapes

Encourage more involved patterns to develop as their experience grows.
'The oval plate could be better set out. How would you do it?'

- ▲ **Producing a bar chart.** The three jellies represent three flavours. Decide what the children think these are, then use cubes to build up a tower to find out the favourite flavour in the class. Follow this up by producing a graph. Give the children squares of paper, girls yellow, boys green. They draw themselves and write their names on the square, then arrange them above the jelly of their choice.

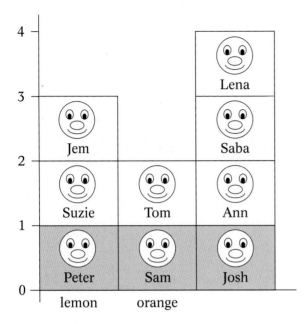

They can use their graph to answer lots of questions.

Similar graphs could be produced using the ice creams and ice lollies.

In mixed age classes you could produce a birthday cake graph showing the number of candles on your last cake.

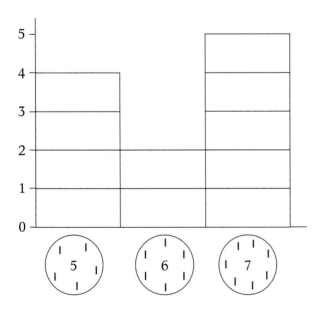

- **Introducing fractions.** Simple fractions can be introduced using the sandwich plate. Cutting rolls in half to be filled with chosen favourite foods, cutting cakes and pizzas into 2, 4 etc will provide opportunities to demonstrate and discuss simple fractions.

Simple recording ideas

- Children can draw or write their favourite flavours on paper plates or food shapes.

▲ Cut out pieces of coloured sugar paper to represent plates and use sponge shapes with paint to print food patterns on them.

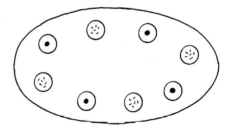

● Use a birthday cake to explore pattern and co-ordination skills. Draw a faint pattern on the cake for children to colour, and let them cut out and stick on candles.

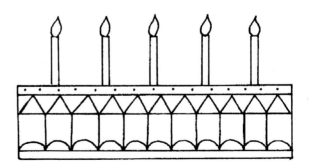

■ Set out a table of real or pretend party food, and work with a group of up to six children to give experience of addition and subtraction. The activity could begin as a game using a standard dice, or dice marked (0, 1, 2, 0, 1, 2). Take it in turn to roll the dice and choose items from the table to put on to their own plates. After 2 or 3 turns players count the items of food on their plates. The winner is the person with the most items, or least if you prefer. Alternatively the winner could be the first to collect 10 items of food. Many variations may be suggested by the children.

Jasper
4 items

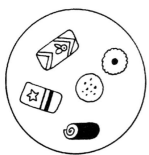

Farah
5 items

Lucy
9 items

Using the border

■ **Finding sets.** Cover each set of items with counters or cubes, then count them. Find the pairs of blowers and sweets.

▲ **Use the numbers** (2, 3, 4, 5) as a starting point for investigations.

Invite children to draw items to match the four numbers – anything they like, or items from the mat.

2 cakes

3 cookies

4 lollies

5 ices

Talk about the pictures. For example:
There are more ices than lollies.
There are fewer cakes than cookies.
There are twice as many lollies as cakes.
There are 3 more ice creams than cakes.

If you put the cakes and cookies together there will be 5 things.

● **Making totals.** Use any of the numbers 2, 3, 4, 5 with + to make as many different totals as possible. For example:

$2 + 3 = 5$ $2 + 5 = 7$ $2 + 3 + 5 = 10$

Use other operations to produce different results:

$3 - 2 = 1$ $4 + 3 - 2 = 5$

■ **Exploring numbers.** Use the items in the border as a starting point for investigating numbers.

• Use the blowers to explore 8. There are 4 blowers in the top border, 4 in the lower border $4 + 4 = 8$
There are four pairs of blowers
$2 + 2 + 2 + 2 = 8$ or $4 \times 2 = 8$

Introduce subtraction by covering some of the blowers with a counter or plasticine. For example, cover two: $8 - 2 = 6$

Find different ways to make 8 using items from the border. For example:

$$3 \quad + \quad 3 \quad + \quad 2$$

If you cover these items, what is left? (3 ices, 1 lolly, 8 sweets and 8 blowers)

- Use the sweets or all the ices to investigate 10. Combine items to investigate other numbers. For example, with lollies and blowers you get $4 + 8 = 12$

- Use the side borders to explore 5. You could begin with a story: Here we have 3 ice creams and 2 lollies, five things altogether. What other combinations could we have? (Consider flavours if you want to challenge.)
  5 lollies
  4 lollies and 1 ice
  3 lollies and 2 ices
  2 lollies and 3 ices
  1 lolly and 4 ices
  5 ices

Record you results in an interesting way. For example:

5	(ices and lolly illustration)	4 ices 1 lolly
5	(ices and lollies illustration)	3 ices 2 lollies

- Similar investigations can be stimulated using the 9 items in the upper or lower border.

Extension activities

- **Using money**. Introduce money by giving each item a value, then set problems. For example

10p   2p   20p   15p

- Find the cost of 8 blowers (80p), 10 sweets (20p), 6 ices (£1.20), 4 lollies (60p). What is the total cost? (£2.80)
- If you have, say, 30p to spend, what could you buy? Record all the possibilities.
- Change the values.

Starfish

Mathematical concepts

Number (focus upon number five, pairs), shape (introduce the pentagon; match size, shape etc), data handling, simple probability.

Description of the mat

This mat has been designed to provide children with a stimulus for detailed observation and discussion.

The centre has five starfish, each with five arms. Two are large, three are small. Each arm has a different number (from 1 to 4) of pads. These can be counted by covering them with small counters or cubes. These can be used for counting beyond 10 and could provide stimulus for considering simple multiplication. There are:

Small Starfish 3, 3, 2, 2, 2, total 12
                        3, 1, 2, 3, 1, total 10
                        1, 1, 2, 2, 2, total 8
Large Starfish 4, 4, 3, 4, 2, total 17
                        3, 3, 3, 2, 2, total 13

The background shows a selection of sea shells and sea creatures; children should be encouraged to look for similarities and differences. These will provide a good talking point. Most children will benefit from discussing in some detail what they see, before practical work begins.

The four sections of the border each contain a number of shells, which may be used for sorting by covering similar shells with counters.

As the shells are drawn from various directions lengthy discussion may be needed to decide which are similar. A set of real shells would be very helpful.

The corners each contain a pentagon with a star inside, coloured in different ways. These will provide an opportunity to discuss the features of a regular pentagon. Children can trace over the starfish shapes and the pentagons to develop shape work.

Useful resources

A collection of shells for matching and counting; books that illustrate shells so that children can find out the names of the different shells shown; Starfish resource sheet.

Teacher's notes

Using the starfish

- ■ **General discussion.** Encourage observation of the various creatures. There is potential for counting the number of starfish, the shells, animals, etc.

- ▲ **Looking at the shape.** Use fingers to draw round the shape of one of the large starfish.

- ● **Counting pads.** Match small counters onto the pads and count. The total may be recorded inside the star fish.

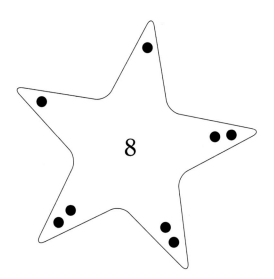

- ■ **Making the same number.** Draw in extra pads on a starfish so that there are the same number on each arm.

- ▲ **Making starfish.** Cut out paper or card starfish for each child and provide sticky circle shapes to use as pads. Tell them how many pads to put on the starfish.

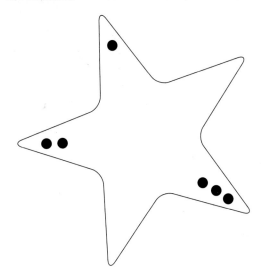

'Put 6 pads on your starfish. Tell us where you have put them.'

- ● **Making 10.** Use two sets of coloured counters and make up totals by making patterns to count and talk about as a group. Work on the starfish with 10 pads.

'Who has used the most red?'
'Who has used the most yellow?'

These could be coloured and displayed, showing the various totals of each colour, say red and yellow:

$0 + 10$, $1 + 9$, $2 + 8$, $3 + 7$, $4 + 6$, $5 + 5$, $6 + 4$, $7 + 3$, $8 + 2$, $9 + 1$, $10 + 0$

- ■ **Starfish: a game for 2 players.** You need a mat for each player, a set of small coloured counters or buttons, and a dice marked 0, 1, 1, 2, 3, 4

The aim of the game is to match counters to the pads on the starfish and be the first player to cover all the pads on your mat. Various restrictions should be imposed depending upon the ability and concentration span of the players.

For example, counters may be placed on only one arm in any turn.

So, if a 4 is rolled, then four counters must be placed on one of the arms with four pads (there are three of these). Once these have been covered if a 4 is rolled you miss that go.

Before play begins it is useful to discuss the number of arms with:

1 pad	4 arms	4
2 pads	10 arms	20
3 pads	8 arms	24
4 pads	3 arms	12
total	25 arms	60 pads

Note: If you roll a 1 this may be placed on any of the arms – it is not necessary to fill the arm on one roll of the dice.

There is a lot of strategy involved in this game once the children get used to it.

Using the border

■ **Matching, sorting and recording**. Using a collection of shells the children could match real shells to the shells in the border. A graph could then be produced using the actual shells on a square grid, showing the number of each shell. This could then be produced as a written recording if appropriate. The children might make up their own collection and sort the appropriate data for recording.

Support activity

Matching and counting. The shells in the border have been drawn to pair up with a shell in the middle so children could cover identical shells with matching counters. They could start by simply counting the shells in each part of the border (from top, clockwise: 8, 5, 6, 4).

The Starfish resource sheet

▲ **Making a number**. You could write a number inside a starfish and invite the children to share that number of counters among the arms.

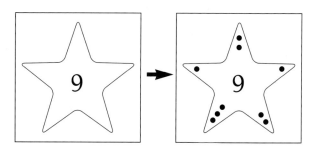

'How many different ways can you find to do this. Begin to record.'

● **Adding numbers.** Vary the activity by putting a number by each arm of the starfish, for children to add the pads, and record the total.

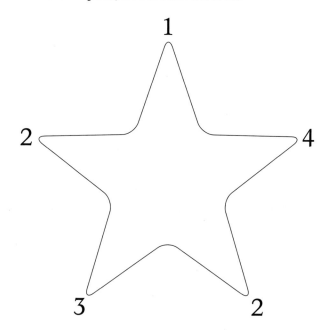

■ **Making patterns.** Colour the pentagons in the border to produce a pattern, or number and then colour them. Use the pentagons to count up to 30. Cover each pentagon with a counter to collect 30 then find how many 'fives' there are in 30 by building towers around the arms of a starfish shape like this.

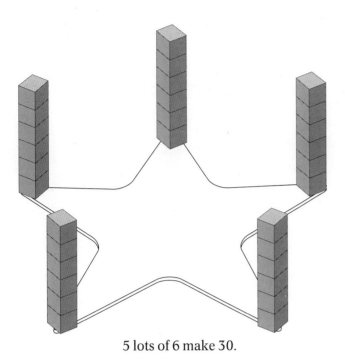

5 lots of 6 make 30.

This provides a good introduction to the concept of sharing and division.

▲ **Collecting shells: a game for 2 players.** You need lots of shells in a basket or open tray, and a dice (numbered 0–5) (or different dice eg 0, 1, 2, 0, 1, 2 or 1, 2, 3, 1, 2, 3)

Match a suitable shell to each shell on the border.

Take it in turns to roll the dice and remove that number of shells from one section of the border. If there are insufficient shells in any section miss the turn.

For example, if the first player rolls 5, 5 shells may be removed from the top, bottom or right hand sections. If the second player then rolls a 5 there are only two sections where the shells can be removed. As play continues it becomes a disadvantage to roll large numbers because you may not be able to remove the shells.

Play continues until all shells have been removed from the border. The winner is the player who has collected the most shells. As there are 23 shells to collect there will inevitably be a winner.

Related work on pentagons and stars

- Look at stars as five pointed shapes.

- Introduce 'pentagon' and make pictures using regular and irregular five sided shapes.

- Make five sided shapes on a pin board.

- Draw some pentagons; measure the sides.

- Make five sided shapes using straws and pipecleaners or geostrips.

- Use pentagons from Polydron or Clixi to produce 2D and 3D shapes.

- Ask the children to make up a game using the pentagon shapes around the border of the resource sheet.

- A simple number line could be produced in the resource sheet border, highlighting multiples of 5 with a different colour.

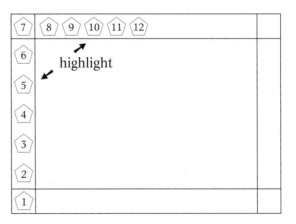

Starfish

Name...

NCM Module 2 Games

Money

20p	45p	12p	35p	53p	70p	25p	80p	50p
72p								23p
65p								15p
21p								27p
32p								60p
17p	1p	2p	5p	10p	20p	50p	£1	56p
£1	57p	24p	40p	75p	30p	11p	52p	10p

Mathematical concepts

Coin recognition, making sums of money with coins; sorting, matching, data handling; investigation and problem sorting with values of coins and combinations of coins.

Description of the mat

The mat is designed so that coins valued at 1p, 2p, 5p, 10p, 20p, 50p and £1 can be sorted into the columns marked.

Various values are shown in the border, using colour combinations, to stimulate investigation and problem solving. The corners highlight the values of the highest value coins used on the mat.

Useful resources

Coins of each denomination shown; large coloured counters; a selection of dice; calculators.

Teacher's notes

A large tray of money is essential for working with this mat. Several copies of the mat would be very useful.

If you work with groups of 8–10 children you will be able to assess each child's ability to identify and understand the values of coins. Children may work individually or in pairs.

- **Sorting.** To reinforce the basic skill of recognising coins, invite each child to select 5 coins from the tray and sort the coins onto the grid. For example,

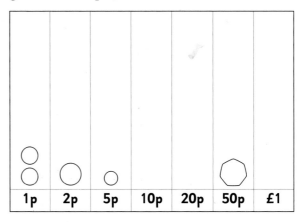

$$50p + 5p + 2p + 1p + 1p = 59p$$

This activity should be repeated using different restrictions:

- Choose 5 different coins.
- Choose coins that total more than 80p.
- Choose coins that total exactly 50p.
- Choose coins that total less than £1.
- Choose only bronze (silver) coins.

▲ **Making 20p.** To focus on the values of coins, children could place coins of a set total in each of the columns, eg twenty 1p coins, ten 2p coins, four 5p coins, two 10p coins and one 20p coin respectively in the first five columns.

● **Exploring totals.** Explore totals using various rules, eg total 5 coins of the same value; what are the possible totals you can get?

$$1p + 1p + 1p + 1p + 1p = 5p$$
$$10p + 10p + 10p + 10p + 10p = 50p, \text{ etc}$$

■ **How many coins do you need?** Invite children to solve the problem of manipulating coin values to produce a total amount. Choose any of the values around the border, say 27p. Mark it with a counter or pointer made from felt or paper.

20p		50p
		→ ⚡27p
£1		10p

Each member of the group should collect coins from the tray to total 27p and sort these onto their mat. When everyone has done this, the various solutions should be discussed. You could ask:

'Who has used the least number of coins? Could it be done using less?'

'Who has used the most coins? Could you do it with more?'

You could set most groups some of the following challenges while you work with other groups.

Using the border

■ **Making amounts with coins.** Lay the mat in the centre of the carpet or a large table. Ask children to collect coins that total each of the amounts shown around the border then stack the coins on top of the total or lay them alongside or under each value like this.

10p + 5p + 2p

◎		
£1	⚡57p	⚡24p

50p   20p
5p   2p
2p   2p

(If you have only one mat ask individual children to do a particular set, eg the labels with orange on yellow or yellow on green.)

Further challenges

• Is it possible to make each value using a maximum of 3 coins? (yes)

• Which totals can be made using several coins of the same value, eg
40p ↔ 20p + 20p
25p ↔ 5p + 5p + 5p + 5p + 5p

• Use large counters to cover all the money values greater than 30p but less than 50p. (... more than 70p ...)

• Can you cover two amounts that together total £1 or 70p ...

• Set out coins in the grid that total, say, 65p. Challenge the children to find the total and cover that value in the border with a counter.

Exchange: A game for 4, 6 or 8 players to develop the concept of exchanging coins. You need a mat or a money grid resource sheet for each pair, a dice (1–6) and a large tray of coins.

Players work in pairs. The aim of the game is to be the first pair to collect £2 as two £1 coins on the grid. (The total may be varied according to the ability of the group. One 50p may be appropriate or even one 20p.)

Take it in turns to roll the dice and collect the score in pence. For example, if you score 6 collect 6p; this may be taken as
3 × 2p
5p + 1p or
6 × 1p.
One partner should collect the coins, the other sorts them onto the grid and makes exchanges before the dice is rolled on your next turn.

If a pair has ten 2p coins, these may be exchanged for a 20p coin, two 10p coins, or a 10p and two 5p coins. Play continues until a pair have achieved the agreed target.

Value dice, for example 2p, 5p, 10p, 20p, 50p, £1, may be substituted for the 1–6 dice for children who are still working on recognition. Then the game could be adapted so that their aim is to collect at least 6 of each coin. This introduces simple exchange.

Other games may be created using the money grid and the border.

NB Exchange between pairs of columns varies. You will need to discuss this.

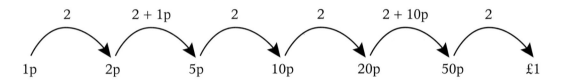

Extension activities

■ **Adding pairs in the border**. Challenge the children to total pairs of amounts round the border, using a calculator to help. They can make their own 'flashes' to record their answers by cutting several scraps of paper at the same time.

25p	80p	**50p**

73p

23p

38p

15p

42p

27p

87p

60p

£1.16

56p

As there are an odd number of values on each side, these maybe combined in two ways as shown here.
Once each group has set out their totals they could check them with another group, rechecking those where they disagree.
You may need to discuss values of over 100.

Which totals come to over £1? (Vary the amount to suit the children.)

▲ **Making totals.** Find pairs to total set amounts, eg less than £1.
Record your findings on a large 100 square.

77	78	79	80
65p + 12p	57p + 21p	52p + 27p	45p + 35p
87	**88**	**89**	**90**
75p + 12p	65p + 23p	65p + 24p	75p + 15p
97	**98**	**99**	**100**
65p + 32p	75p + 23p	75p + 24p	

● **Giving change**. Investigate change given from £1 for some or all of the values in the border. Lay out the change in a stack on the value or spread alongside it.

1p	2p	5p	10p	20p	50p	£1

Money grid

Name...

NCM Module 2 Games © Cambridge University Press 1995

Town map

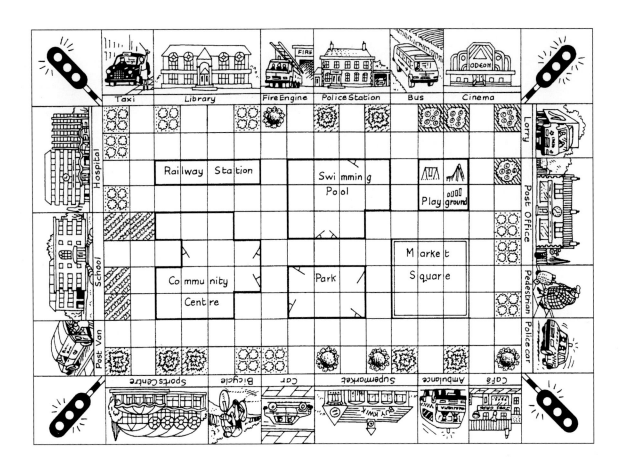

Mathematical concepts

Number development, counting; mapping routes, sequencing and ordering, direction; introducing appropriate language of position (left, right, near, far, next to) simple area (size and shape), simple vocabulary of length leading to perimeter.

Description of the mat

This mat is brightly coloured and has a birds-eye view plan layout in the centre of the mat showing:

The railway station	(4 square units)
A swimming pool	(11 square units)
The playground	(4 square units)
A community centre	(13 square units)
The park	(6 square units)
The market square	(9 square units).

There are paths/roads within the grid and a variety of environmental features marked at the entrance to the pictures around the border.

 Seven trees

 Ten clusters of bushes

 Four trees surrounded by small bushes

 Four rose bushes with pink flowers

 Four sets of small plants

The border

Around the four sides there are places marked with yellow labels and modes of transport marked with pink labels.

	Modes of Transport	Size in units	Buildings/places	Size in units
Top border	Taxi	2	Library	4
	Fire engine	2	Police station	3
	Bus	2	Cinema	3
Right side	Lorry	2	Post office	4
	Pedestrian	2		
	Police car	2		
Lower border	Ambulance	2	Café	2
	Car	2	Supermarket	4
	Bicycle	2	Sports centre	4
Left side	Post van	2	School	4
			Hospital	4

The corners show the sequence of four combinations of lights on a traffic light. Lights that are on are indicated by flash marks.

Red, red and amber, green, amber.

Useful resources

Counters, for moving around the centre square grid, squared paper, compass for direction marking (north, south, east, west), sticks of equal length.

Teacher's notes

■ **General discussion**. This mat is particularly detailed. Encourage children to observe and apply mathematical knowledge to each section. It is intended that children focus upon identifying the number and shape of features for reinforcement, for example:

Which buildings have a clock (chimneys, circular windows)?
Which buildings occupy 3 units (4 units, 2 units)?
Which buildings have roses near the entrance?

Which buildings have triangles in their design?

Interpretation can result from discussion. For example:

Where would you go to spend money (buy stamps, bread, etc)?

What happens in the hospital (school, post office)?

▲ **Journeys.** Introduce the idea of journeys and travelling from one place to another. This may be done in a variety of ways:

• Start at a set place, say the supermarket.

'How far is it to the café?'
Count the square units using a counter to get there. (8 squares, no cutting corners!)

'How far will the police car go to get to the police station by the shortest route?'
(15 squares)
'How far is the ambulance from the hospital?'
(20 squares)

• Plan simple two stage journeys as a means of counting and planning appropriate routes.

For example:

'Take the taxi to the supermarket and then on to the park for lunch . How far have you travelled?'

Remember there are always going to be several possible answers, each are equally valid and should be considered.

- You could use this mat as a stimulus for story telling to develop the idea of sequencing and logic. Tell a story about a day out using some of the features of the map. The cyclist, for example, could provide a focus for discussion of a journey through the community centre, to the swimming pool and then to the park.

● **Relationships.** Describe some of the relationships between the buildings and the types of transport shown.
The hospital is near to the library, next to the school, far away from the café and post office. The ambulance is likely to go to the hospital! Why?

▲ **Size.** The idea of size could be introduced through discussion, using the square units to compare each building or area.
The community centre takes up more area than the park.
The swimming pool takes up less area than the community centre.

● **Compass directions.** Once the children are familiar with the map they could move round it following directions using points of the compass, north, south, east and west. Position the mat and label north. Give directions for getting from one place to another to encourage problem solving.

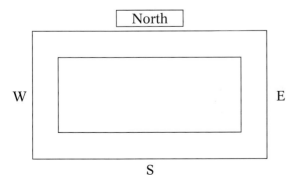

Activities to follow on from the discussion work

■ **Area.** The swimming pool covers 11 units. What other shapes could it have been? There are many possibilities, such as:

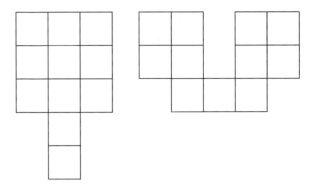

Which of these shapes are 'sensible' for such a building?

Investigate the size of other market squares and are they always square?

Draw a town plan of your own. Use squared paper, ruler and pencil.

▲ **Investigate routes** around the town map, for example:

What buildings would you expect to pass en route by bus to the sports centre?

Describe the journey you would take from the police station to the school. Use 'forwards', 'left', 'right'.

● **Perimeter.** Investigate the perimeter of each of the buildings and places in the centre of the map.

Then using some units of length such as lollipop sticks or standard pencils, make some plans of buildings or places.

It is 8 units round the playground.

It is 12 units of length around the market square.

Here is another 'shape' that measures 12 units around the outside (perimeter).

■ **Pattern**. The traffic lights are a useful focus for pattern work and sequencing pattern.

The order of the sequence should be talked about and the children could record the sequence that occurs on actual traffic lights, using counters to represent the three colours.

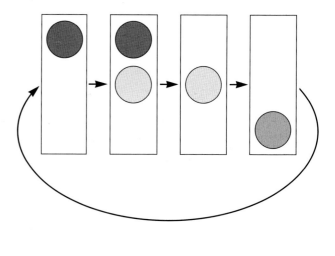

Hundred square

Mathematical concepts

Number recognition, matching, ordering, sorting, more than, less than, introduction to tens and units; number pattern; grid work.

Description of the mat

This mat is included as a support mat to introduce children to larger numbers. The numbers 1 to 100 are placed as a child would read a page, from left to right and top to bottom.

The border incorporates symbols for addition, subtraction and multiplication and the four corners are marked with the easier multiple patterns ($\times 2, \times 3, \times 10, \times 5$).

Useful resources

A photocopiable A4 copy of the 100 square is included for follow-up work or individual reference.

Counters, spirit pens, dice, cubes and calculators. Strips of card 20 cm long and 2 cm wide would be useful for targeting sections of the 100 grid. These can be used to cover up particular numbers or to highlight blocks of numbers.

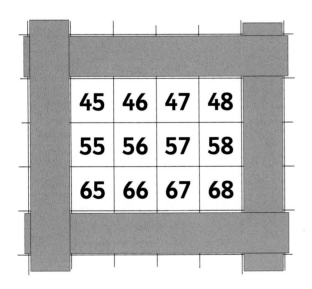

Teacher's notes

This mat can be used for stimulation and discussion. Children in year 1 need to become familiar with large numbers, and to talk about, recognise, and locate numbers. Familiarity with the 100 square will enable children to identify tens and units families and to begin to spot number patterns. All types of grids may be created once children become aware of the value of sorting numbers and ordering them in some way.

There will be many times when a 100 square will be useful. The mat can be displayed on the wall for quick reference.

Using the 100 square

- **Preliminary discussion**. Read the numbers. Cover particular numbers with a counter, and ask the children to tell you which number is covered.
  Ask children to describe the location of numbers, using the words 'row' and 'column': '63 is in row 7.' '96 is in row 10.' '54 is in column 4.' etc.

  Tell me 3 numbers in column 5 ... (45, 55, 85)
  Which numbers are either side of 65 ?
  (64 and 66)
  Which numbers are above and below 53 ?
  (43, 63)

- ▲ **Tens and units.** Begin to introduce the language of tens and units.

  Find the number made of 2 tens and 8 units, etc. (28)
  Show me the numbers with 7 units ...
  Show me the numbers with 8 tens (point to the rows or columns)
  Find a number which has 5 tens and 5 units (55), 6 tens and 6 units (66). Where are these positioned on the 100 square? Can you see a pattern?

- **Counting on and back**. Use the grid for counting on and back to discover numbers greater than, or less than a selected number. For example, count on from 65 to add 5. How many? (70)
Tell me a number greater than 63 but less than 70, etc.

- **Generating sums.** The 100 square can be used for generating calculations. For example, choose any pair of neighbouring numbers; use a calculator to find out what you get if you add them together. Can you find this number on the 100 square?

    $6 + 7 = 13$ $18 + 19 = 37$

Choose any two numbers at random and add them together.

- **Making 20**. Try to find two numbers that make 20 if you add them together. ($16 + 4$, $7 + 13$, etc.) How many pairs can you find?

- **Making their own squares**. Once the children are familiar with the organisation of a grid encourage them to draw their own and fill it with numbers. This can generate good assessment activities with groups or a class. For example, draw a 4×4 grid. (The size and shape of the grid can be varied to provide the appropriate number of spaces.)
How many squares are there?
Give the group instructions, using relevant language (words of position, random numbers from a specified set, shapes) gradually to fill the grid with information. Observe the children as they complete the tasks and follow the instructions to assess understanding.

For example:

12	4	6	9
16	18	23	27
28	8	58	38
7	20	10	33

Write a number 12 in the top left-hand corner box.
Write number 33 in the lower right-hand corner.
Put the number 10 in the box to the left of number 33.
These three tasks are extremely useful in assessing children's basic knowledge and understanding.

The following are more complex instructions to challenge more able pupils.
Write four numbers greater than 15 but less than 30 in the four boxes in the second row.
Fill the three empty boxes in the 2nd column with **even** numbers.
Put three more numbers in the 3rd row that have 8 units (28, 38, 58)
Put an odd number less than 10 in the space in column one.
Write two numbers that total 15 in the remaining two spaces.
There are very many variations of this activity.
Adapt your questions to check relevant maths concepts and provide adequate challenge for your children.

- **Ordering numbers.** Prepare numbers written in words on cards and a line of boxes. Ask children to order the numbers and record them in order on a long grid.

| thirteen | eight | twenty | fourteen | twenty-four | eleven | four | seventeen |

You could suggest that they cover the numbers on the 100 grid to find the order.

Using the border

- **Introducing the symbols for addition, subtraction and multiplication.** The use of the calculator will help children to recognise and understand the different effects of each sign. Talk about +, – and × signs. Cover over each of the signs with a large cube or counter. Lift a cube and ask children to describe the sign. Introduce the variety of words used and associated with each sign.

  +: add, addition, total

  –: take away, subtract, minus, difference

  ×: multiply, times, sets of.

- ▲ **Pairs: an activity for 2 or 3 players.** You need large counters or blocks.
  Look carefully at the location of each sign before covering them all up. Take it in turns to uncover two signs to try to find two the same. Replace the counters/cubes if they are different. This is useful in learning to differentiate between + and ×.

- ● **Sign trail:** a game for 2 to 4 players. You need counters, a 1–6 dice and a calculator for each player.

Each player places a counter on the × 10 corner square and starts off with 10 points entered into their calculator.
Take it in turns to roll the dice and move that number of spaces. Everyone makes one full circuit. If you land on a sign (+, –, ×) roll the dice again and carry out the appropriate calculation with your points and the score.
For example, Jared starts with 10 points. He rolls 6, moves from × 10 to –. He rolls the dice, scores 3 and so subtracts 3 from his 10 points, ending up with 7.
If you land on a blank, play continues without change of your score. If you land on a corner, you multiply your existing score by either 3, 5 or 2 as appropriate. You must roll the exact score to finish on × 10, and then multiply your points total by 10 (so 37 becomes 370 total). The winner is the player with the greatest total. This game can be varied to match the ability of the children playing. For example, omit the corner squares with the less able.

Hundred square

Name...

1	2	3	4	5	6	7	8	9	10
11	12	13	14	15	16	17	18	19	20
21	22	23	24	25	26	27	28	29	30
31	32	33	34	35	36	37	38	39	40
41	42	43	44	45	46	47	48	49	50
51	52	53	54	55	56	57	58	59	60
61	62	63	64	65	66	67	68	69	70
71	72	73	74	75	76	77	78	79	80
81	82	83	84	85	86	87	88	89	90
91	92	93	94	95	96	97	98	99	100

Playing cards

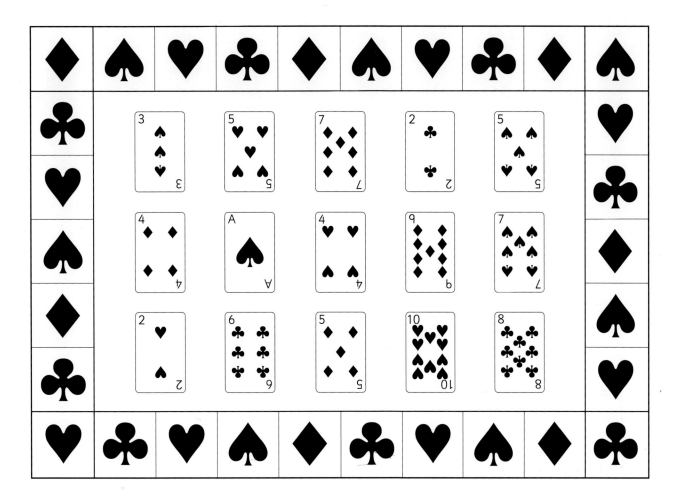

Mathematical concepts

Addition, subtraction, multiplication, mental calculation, estimation, number investigation and problem solving; sorting, ordering, data handling; reinforcement of number recognition, matching, sorting.

Description of the mat

This mat is designed to be particularly versatile in obtaining general information about children's numeracy skills. It provides an introduction to the mathematics that can be developed from a set of 52 playing cards. A selection of 15 cards are shown.

The advantage of the mat is that the cards will remain 'still' whilst you use them for discussion and mental calculation, but it is recommended that a full set of cards be available for use during these activities.

The illustration shows only number cards, and the four suits are arranged so that all are included in one row and one or more are missing from the other rows and columns.

The border contains a repeating pattern of heart, club, diamond, spade, starting in a clockwise direction from the bottom left corner and ending with a club.
A range of games could be played using this border.

Cards	spades	hearts	diamonds	clubs	red total	black total	total
row 1	2	1	1	1	2	3	5
row 2	2	1	2	0	3	2	5
row 3	0	2	1	2	3	2	5
total	4	4	4	3	8	7	15

Value	spades	hearts	diamonds	clubs	red total	black total	total
row 1	3 + 5	5	7	2	12	10	22
row 2	1 + 7	4	4 + 9	0	17	8	25
row 3	0	2 + 10	5	6 + 8	17	14	31
total					46	32	

Value	column 1	column 2	column 3	column 4	column 5
	3	5	7	2	5
	4	1	4	9	7
	2	6	5	10	8
total	9	12	16	21	20

Useful resources

Counters, cubes, dice, playing cards, calculators; small counting objects, bears, blocks etc.

Teacher's notes

■ **General discussion.** The chosen range of cards will provide the teacher with a good starting point for many aspects of number work. As with all mats children must have plenty of time to talk about the mat and what they see.

Prompt them with questions like:

'Can you find an ace?'
'How many 2s can you see?' (2)
'Can you find the seven of spades?'

Explore the mat for totals for rows/columns/sets of cards/colour etc.

'How many red cards?' (8)
'What is the total number of spades?' (4)
'Are there more hearts or clubs?' (hearts)
'What is the total in the first column?' (9)
'What is the total in the top row?' (22)

Using a full set of playing cards

■ **Sorting**. Children who would benefit from sorting activities could sort a pack of cards by colour, or suit, or number and picture.

▲ **Matching**. It is important to do lots of practical matching. Lay out cards and put the appropriate number of objects alongside or below.

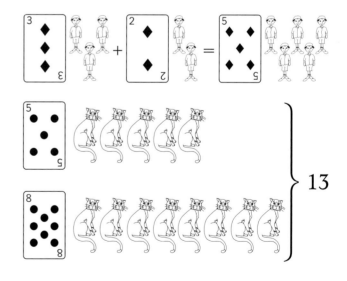

Record your results in as many ways as possible.

- **Ordering.** Children could order the number cards 1–10 in one suit. Then secretly remove one card and challenge them to tell you which card has been taken.

- **Making totals.** Ask children to find pairs of cards (or sets of 3, 4, or 5 cards) to make a total. For example find sets of three cards with a total of 15.
  Alternatively, if they total each set of cards with the same number, they will gain experience of multiples of four.

Using the cards in the centre

- **Matching and comparing.** Use the mat with a small group or have a number of mats for use individually or in pairs.
  Provide the children with counters, cubes etc and match objects to the number on each of the 15 cards. Discuss which cards have more/less/the same number.

- ▲ **Make a number.** Set a total and challenge the children to add enough objects to each card to make the total.

  For example, make 10.

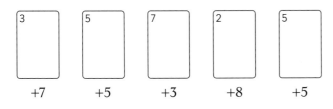

- **Comparing and differences.** Explore more, less and difference using the cards. For example, put the matching number of counters on a card. Transfer the correct number to another card. Look at how many more there are left on the first card.

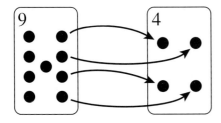

- **Subtraction.** Take away 3 from each of the numbers on the mat. Discuss what happens when you reach the 2 of clubs (–1; you have to borrow one).

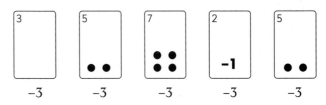

- ▲ **Multiples.** Start to explore multiples. Build sets onto a card, for example:

  Add 4 cubes each time you count another set.
  1 set of 4 = 4
  2 sets of 4 = 8
  3 sets of 4 = 12

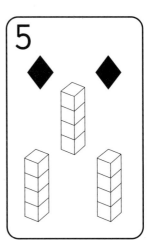

- **Investigating targets and totals.** If it is possible to get a set of large playing cards, these are a good stimulus for group work.

  Select 3 cards.

Challenge the children to combine the cards in as many ways as possible to produce different results. For example:

7 + 5 – 4 = 8
4 + 5 – 7 = 2
7 + 4 – 5 = 6

There are lots more, especially if the numbers may be combined like this.

74 – 5 = 69
75 + 4 = 79   etc.

A calculator will help the children to explore these larger numbers. Encourage them to estimate by inviting them to perform a calculation giving them a result as near to a set total as possible. For example, using 9, 5 and 3 try to make 11.

9 + 3 = 12
5 + 5 + 3 = 13
9 – 3 + 5 = 11   *This is exactly 11! Well done!*
9 + 5 – 3 = 11   *This works as well. Great!*

Games using the border

■ **Three in a row: a shape and logic game for 2 players.** You need a pack of cards, two sets of coloured counters and paper and pencil for keeping score.

Shuffle the cards and put them in a pile face down in the middle of the mat. Each player chooses a colour for their counters.

Take turns to pick up the top card, identify the suit and put one of your counters on any of that symbol in the border. Once placed, a counter may not be moved, and only one counter can be put on each symbol.

The aim of the game is to collect the most points. Points are scored by covering three symbols in a row, either along a side, or round a corner.

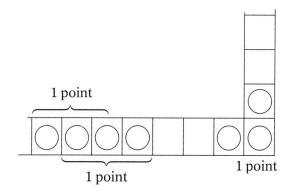

1 point

1 point

1 point

If you can put another counter at one end of your row when you have another turn, you score another point.

You can try to block your opponent's rows where possible.

The winner is the player with most points when play ends. This could be when all symbols are covered, or when players have used all their counters (limit the number to, say, 10). For a shorter game, the winner is first to score, say, 3 points.

▲ **Four family fun: a game for 3 to 4 players.** You need a pack of cards with the picture cards removed, a dice and a counter or coloured marker for each player.

Shuffle the cards and deal 7 to each player. Sort the remaining cards into four piles by suit. Put the piles face down, with the king of each suit beside the pile to show its suit.

The aim of the game is to collect a family of four cards either the same number, for example all the 4s, or a run in the same suit, for example 2, 3, 4, 5 of clubs or 6, 7, 8, 9 of hearts.

Each put your marker on one of the four corners to start. Take turns to roll the dice and move that number of spaces round the board. Whatever suit you land on, pick up the top card from that pile (land on a diamond, collect a diamond). Once a card is selected it may be kept or discarded face up onto the 'king pile' for other players to collect when it is their turn. If the card is kept the player must put down another card so that players retain only 7 cards at a time. You may only pick up a card when it is your turn to play, and you may only pick up the top card from a pile.

This game helps children to sort and order, and use logical thinking; they need to stay alert and remember which cards have been discarded.

● **Cover up: a game for 3 to 4 players.** You need 15 pieces of card (4 cm × 6 cm) to cover the cards on the mat, a dice (1–6), a counter or coloured marker for each player, a set of counters or calculator for each player to keep score.

Each put your marker on one of the four corners to begin the game.

Take it in turns to roll the dice and move that number of places round the board. Look at the suit you land on. Choose a card of that suit on the mat, score the number of points then cover over the card. For example,

Carla lands on a diamond. She decides to cover the 7 of diamonds and therefore scores 7 points.

If all the cards of your suit have been covered, you cannot cover up and score.

The aim of the game is to be the first player to reach an agreed target total, eg 20.

This is a great matching game, and encourages understanding of number value.

Calendar

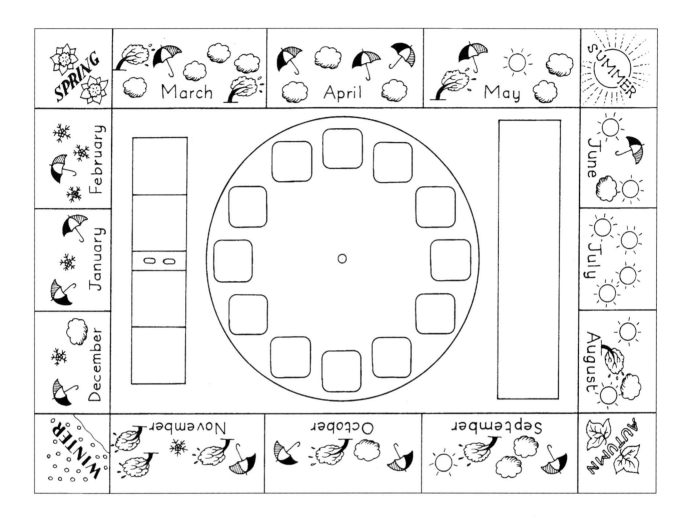

Mathematical concepts

Time, seasons, months of the year; data handling.

Description of the mat

The mat is intended mainly as a resource for discussion work. The clock outline in the centre has twelve boxes marked so that the appropriate numbers can be drawn in by teacher or pupil using a spirit pen, or numbers from the resource sheet can be added with Blu-Tack. The two rectangular boxes are for recording analogue time (eg 3 o'clock) or digital time (eg 10:30), or other notes.

The months of the year are drawn in order round the border, grouped in blocks with seasons in the preceding corners.

Autumn	September, October, November
Winter	December, January, February
Spring	March, April, May
Summer	June, July, August

Each month has weather symbols to indicate the most usual weather during the month. The more symbols, the more sunshine, wind, rain, cloud or snow expected.

Weather chart	rain	cloud	sunshine	wind	snow
January	2				1
February	1				3
March	1	4		2	
April	3	3			
May	1	2	1	1	
June	1	1	2		
July			4		
August		1	2	1	
September	1	2	1	1	
October	2	1		1	
November	1			3	1
December	1	1			1
total	14	15	10	9	6

Useful resources

Counters, Times and dates resource sheets.

Teacher's notes

Activities using the centre of the mat

■ **A classroom resource.** This mat could be used as a permanent reference resource in the classroom. Special times could be drawn onto the clock and a message written in the box. Display the mat near the actual clock for children to match the time to the working clock. Dates could also be fixed by the appropriate month using Blu-Tack and changed daily.

▲ **Using the numbers.** Copy the Times and dates resource sheet onto thin card. Cut out the clock numbers and position them round the clock. Remove one and ask which one is missing.

Turn all the numbers face down on the clock face. Point to a card and ask which number it is. Turn it over then point to another until all 12 cards are face up.

With all the numbers face down, turn over, say, 10 and ask which number is opposite. (4)

These activities will help the children to become more familiar with the lay out of the clock face and aware of the relative positions of the 12 points.

- **Counting on and back.** You can use the numbers round the clock face for simple counting on and back:
'Which number is 3 more than 6?'
Count on round the clock face.

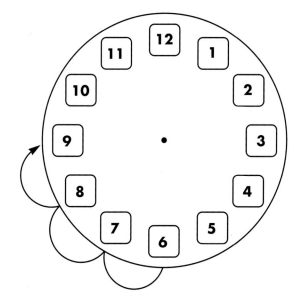

'Which number is 2 less than 10?'

Using the border

- **Discussion.** Children should focus on the weather represented for each month. Talk about the seasons and the weather we might expect. This could provide a context for extending vocabulary of quantity: most, least, greatest amount, small amount, very little rain, a lot of snow, etc. Vary the question according to the group. For example:

'Put a counter on the months that have rain.'
'Put a counter on the months that have sunshine and wind.'
'How many months have no rain?'
'Which months have the most rain / least snow?'
'Which months have rain and snow?'
'Which months have cloud and no sunshine?'
'Describe the weather shown in July, November, April, February, . . .'

As the children use the calendar they will become more familiar with the order of the months. The mat could be a useful poster for the classroom.

- ▲ **Drawing graphs.** Record the number of months that have snow, sunshine, rain, etc and make a weather graph.

- **Around the year:** a game for 3 to 4 players. You need a set of month cards for each player, a mat each.

Put all the month cards into a box and mix them.

The aim of the game is to collect one of each of the twelve months and match them onto your mat. You can extend the game by adding sets of season cards.

Take it in turns to pick a month card out of the box without looking. If you take a month you already have, return the repeat card to the box and that ends your turn.

Support activity

- ■ **Ordering months.** The month cards could be set out in order, using the mat for reference.

Times and dates

Copy and cut out to use with the clock face.

✂

1	2	3	4	5	6
7	8	9	10	11	12

✂

1st	2nd	3rd	4th	5th	6th	7th
8th	9th	10th	11th	12th	13th	14th
15th	16th	17th	18th	19th	20th	21st
22nd	23rd	24th	25th	26th	27th	28th
29th	30th	31st				

✂

Half past	Quarter past	Quarter to	o'clock

1	2	3	4	5	6	7	8	9	10	11	12

Times and dates

January	February	March
April	May	June
July	August	September
October	November	December

Spring	Summer	Autumn	Winter

January	February	March
April	May	June
July	August	September
October	November	December

Spring	Summer	Autumn	Winter

January	February	March
April	May	June
July	August	September
October	November	December

Spring	Summer	Autumn	Winter

The school fete

Mathematical concepts

Number investigation; comparison of number, ordering; multiples of 5 and 10; sorting; simple data handling.

Description of the mat

The mat has been designed to provide opportunities for number investigation. There are three main stalls: the target clown with six holes to throw bean bags through, numbered 2, 3, 4, 5, 7, and 8; the tower of tins with 4, 3, 2 and 1 tins; the tombola with ten gifts numbered as follows: cake 40, plant 50, doll 60, vase 70, ball 80, teddy 45,

bottle 55, sweets 65, car 75, robot 85. There are also 26 people in the picture.

The border contains various items which can be used for counting, data handling and recording: 2 sets of three bean bags (yellow, orange and blue); 4 pairs of balls; a random selection of 10 two-digit numbers sorted by colour.

	green	blue	pink
	80	28	19
	50	56	45
	64		33
			43
			71
Total	194	84	211

Useful resources

This mat could be used in conjunction with the 100 square mat for recording or simply number matching. Counters and calculators, books of raffle tackets and a tombola drum would be useful.

Teacher's notes

Using the clown target

- **Problem solving.** The clown provides good opportunities for problem solving to encourage mental calculation, number manipulation and estimation, and logic.
  - If you are given 6 bean bags to throw and you score with 4. What are the possible totals?
  - I score 10 with 3 bags. How many different ways could I have done this? (2, 3, 5 or 4, 4, 2, etc)
  - I have scored with 4 bean bags, no two bags scored the same total. What could my score be?
  - I have scored only 3s, and 8s with four of the bags. What could my total be? (12, 17, 22, 27, 32)
  - I want a score of 20 with four bags. What should I aim for? (8, 8, 2, 2, or 5, 5, 5, 5, etc)

Using the tower of tin cans

- **Triangle numbers.** Whilst the formal experience of the triangular number pattern may be covered later the initial experience is best gained by building the tower using bricks or cans. Challenge the children to build the pattern for themselves using any appropriate resources available to them.

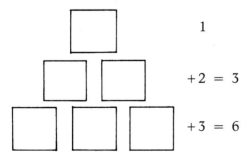

Focus upon the pattern and develop activities to reinforce the image produced.

Use circles to reproduce the pattern then draw this pattern using stencils or sticky paper shapes. Print brick patterns using rectangular sponges. This will help children to recognise the pattern when it occurs.

Using the tombola

- **Multiples of five and ten.** Talk about the prizes and prize numbers. Find these numbers on the 100 square and mark them with counters or plasticine. This activity develops use of multiples of 5 and 10. Matching the numbers shown with the numbers on the 100 square would provide children with an opportunity to find other multiples of 5 or 10 not shown. Writing the number patterns will help to reinforce numbers in both families.

Put the items in numerical order and record the numbers.

40	45	50	...
cake	bear	plant	...

Using the people

- **Sorting.** There are 20 people in the crowd in the lower part of the mat. They have been drawn so that the faces do not overlap, and counters can be placed over the faces to help with sorting. There are several differences. For example, some have hats, glasses, balloons, ..., some do not. The people can be sorted in some of these ways and used as the basis of various activities, such as making comparisons (Are there more people with hats or with glasses?) or producing bar charts.
  - Mark the set of people wearing glasses.
  - Mark the set of people wearing hats.
  - Mark the set of people with brown hair.
  - Mark the set of people holding balloons.

- ▲ **Guess who: a game for two players.** One player chooses a person in the crowd. Their partner asks questions about one feature at a time to try to find out which person has been selected.

Questions might include:
- Does your person have a hat?
- Does your person have glasses?
- Is your person a male?
- Is your person an adult?
- Does your person have dark hair? etc.

Using the border

- **Adding numbers on the raffle tickets.** In the upper and lower sections of the border 10 coloured raffle tickets display a range of numbers. Use a calculator to combine the numbers to produce as many different totals as possible. Begin by using only two tickets, then three, ...
  - What totals might you obtain combining pairs of pink (blue, green) tickets?
  - What totals might you obtain combining odd numbers?
  - Total all the pink (green, blue) tickets.
  - Can you find three tickets totaling more than 150?

- ▲ **Sorting and ordering** the raffle tickets. Sort and order the numbers:
  highest to lowest;
  odds/evens;
  less than 50/more than 50;
  multiples of 5 etc.
  List the numbers less than 40 and those that are more than 50.

- ● **Finding the closest number.** Identify numbers nearest to a chosen number. For example, which number is nearest to 40/55/75 ...

- **Working with a number.** Finding out all one can about a number is a useful way of learning number facts. Once a child has worked with a number it becomes more familiar to them. Work with a group of 10 children or 10 groups if you choose to do this as a class activity. Allocate numbers or invite each team to select a number from the 10 displayed around the border, and ask them to write as many things as they can about their number. For example, if you choose 56:

56 is even
56 is greater than 50 but less than 60
56 is 7 times 8 or 8×7
56 is two lots of 28
56 is 4 less than 60
56 is 14×4

Some numbers are easier to write about than others.

Practical follow-up work

- **Using the jars.** There are two jars shown at opposite corners: the left-hand jar contains 15 items, the other 12 items. Use marbles and two jars to create puzzles and problems to show 'difference', more than, less than.

  - Make one jar contain twice as many as the other.
  - Make one jar contain 6 less than the other.
  - Make one jar contain 12 more than the other.
  - How many marbles have you put into the jars?

- ▲ **Using the fish bowls.** The two fish bowls in one pair of opposite corners can be used to develop vocabulary of size. The bowl on the right contains one big fish. That on the left contains one small and one medium fish.

  - Investigate numbers in the context of goldfish in bowls. For example, how might you organise 7 fish in two large bowls?

- ● **Using raffle tickets.** A book of raffle tackets can provide many activities involving number manipulation. A calculator would be very useful for these types of task.

- Draw tickets from a drum (or box) and order the set:

| 76 | 88 | 103 |

Start with three and extend the number of tickets if appropriate.

- Use both halves of each page, and find the matching pairs of numbers:

| 81 | 81 | 63 | 63 |

- Find pairs of tickets with a given total, for example:

{100} | 51 | 49 | | 87 | 13 |

- Find pairs with a specified difference, for example 10:

| 55 | 65 |

- Find pairs with a particular relationship, for example one is twice the other:

| 3 | 6 | | 10 | 20 | | 12 | 24 |

- ■ **Convert the play area into a tombola game.** Use old raffle tickets and toys as prizes.

- ▲ **Arranging a school fete** is very hard work but involving children in simple tasks can be especially useful.

Circles

Within the six border sections there are 12 circles divided into halves, quarters and three-quarters. The pieces may be compared, matched to make complete circles, and counted by colour or size.

The four corners show circles split into 2, 4, 6 and 8 pieces and shaded for counting purposes.

Useful resources

Tracing paper; circles of paper, sticky paper, sugar paper, tissue paper or felt; circular objects, templates and stencils; a display of cylindrical containers, coins, wheels, etc; Circles resource sheet.

Teacher's notes

■ **Preliminary discussion.** Count the circles. How many small, big, orange, green etc. Use counters to mark the circles.

Look for circles inside circles. Which circles have one circle inside, two, three, none.

Can you find any circles that are the same in some way? Describe what makes them the same.

Using the circles

■ **Comparing circles.** Collect a circular shape or object, eg the lid of a coffee jar. How many of the circles can you cover with the lid? What is the most you can cover at any one time? Can you find a circular shape that will cover each of the green circles?

▲ **Drawing circles.** Trace over the circles, first using a finger, then with pencil and tracing paper.

Mathematical concepts

Number, simple fractions and fraction vocabulary, shape (circles), sorting, vocabulary of position, size (large, small, smaller), colour.

Description of the mat

This mat has been designed to focus on circles. The 25 circles in the centre are six sizes and eight colours. Some circles are inside others. Children should discuss the location of the different circles, count and compare them for size, and become familiar with the mat before more structured activity takes place.

Set challenges involving drawing circles.

(a) Draw three circles: small, medium, large.

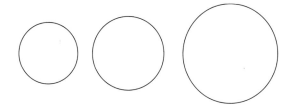

(b) Draw three circles one inside another.

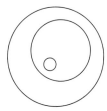

(c) Draw three different sized circles inside a large circle.

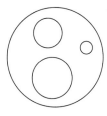

(d) Draw (perhaps using stencils) and cut out 5 different circles using thick paper or card. Make a pattern with these.

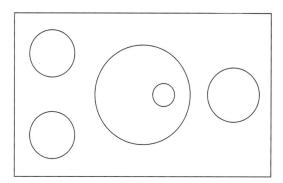

● **Ordering circles.** Cut out a set of different-sized circles. Invite the children to order the circles according to size.

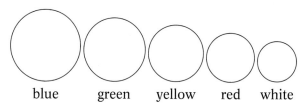

Largest   smallest

blue   green   yellow   red   white

Now ask lots of questions, for example:
'How many circles are larger than the yellow circle?'
'How many are smaller than the blue?'
'What colour is the largest circle?'
'Which circles will fit inside the green circle?'
'Which circles will cover the yellow circle?'

Introducing fractions

■ **Using the border.** Begin to introduce fractions using the border. Introduce the vocabulary half, quarter, three-quarters.
'Cover all the pieces that are this shape.'

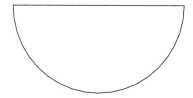

'How many of them do you need to make a whole circle?'

Then work with quarters.

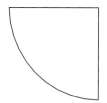

▲ **Using parts of a circle to make a whole.** Cut up circles of felt or paper to produce quarters, halves and three-quarters. Restrict the number of colours to 3 or 4 depending on the variety you wish to create. Play with the pieces to make whole circles.

Set challenges according to the pieces available:

'Use two pieces to make a whole circle.'
'Use three pieces to make a whole circle.'
'Use four pieces.'
'Make a circle using two colours.'
'Make several circles using two pieces for each.'
'Make several circles using three pieces for each.'
The circles resource sheet could be used to record these.

● **Naming and counting fractions.** Use three sets of coloured counters to match the pieces in the border:

quarters, red
halves, yellow
three-quarters, blue

Count the number of each

■ **Combining fractions.** Talk about combinations that will make a whole circle: two halves, one three-quarters plus one quarter, four quarters, one half plus two quarters.

Give each child set of 4 coloured counters. Ask them in turn to cover enough pieces to make a whole circle. Then discuss who achieved this using 2, 3, or 4 counters.

▲ **Making fraction pictures.** Provide the children with glue and paper circles cut into halves, quarters and three-quarters. Invite them to make a picture or pattern using these pieces.

Some might make fraction patterns such as:
$\frac{1}{4}$ $\frac{1}{2}$ $\frac{1}{4}$ $\frac{1}{2}$ $\frac{1}{4}$ etc

These pieces can be used for the following game, Building whole circles.

● **Building whole circles: a game for 2 or 3 players.** You need about 14 different coloured felt or card circles cut into quarters, halves and three-quarters (8 cm diameter gives good sized pieces) in a tray and a six-sided dice marked

$\frac{1}{4}$, $\frac{1}{4}$, $\frac{1}{4}$, $\frac{1}{2}$, $\frac{3}{4}$, $\frac{1}{2}$.

(A large wooden cube can be written on to make this.)

The aim of the game is to collect enough pieces to build **four** whole circles. Decide before you begin whether you must collect each whole in turn or all four at the same time.

Take it in turn to roll the dice then collect an appropriate piece from the tray. The first player to build four complete circles is the winner.

Discuss the ideas and develop the game to extend the children according to their ability.

Using the resource sheet

You could set one group to work on these activities while you work practically with another group. Use the 8 circles on the half resource sheet:

• Draw 8 wheels

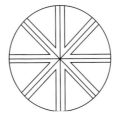 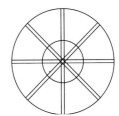

This is good for pattern work.

• Make 8 different faces

Discuss the expressions and feelings.

- Divide into quarters and colour using only two colours. How many different ways can you find?

- Divide into quarters. Write the same number inside each quarter then find the total.

This provides a simple introduction to multiples of 4.

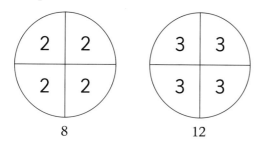

8   12

Alternatively write a random number in each quarter and use a calculator to find the total.

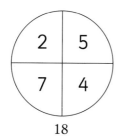

18

- Create other shapes inside each circle.

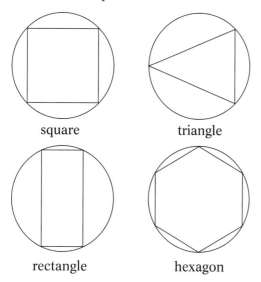

square   triangle

rectangle   hexagon

Challenge more able children to make a star or pentagon.

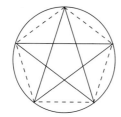

Extension activities

■ **Making whole circles in the border.** Challenge the children to look at each section of the border and total the number of whole circles they can make using the pieces shown. This could be done practically using felt or paper circles.

▲ **Exploring other fractions.** Explore the use of 6 pieces to make a circle, or 8 pieces, as in the two corners of the board.

● **Collecting fractions: a game for 2 to 4 players.** You need the fraction pieces produced for the other game, a 1–6 dice and a coloured counter for each player.

Each put your counter on one of the four corners.

Take it in turn to roll the dice and move around the fraction pieces in the border including the whole circles at each corner.

The aim of the game is to collect a target number of whole circles, for example 4 or 5. (This will depend on how long you want the game to last.)

Collect a piece from the tray to match the size you land on. If you land on a corner, collect a whole circle. Pieces may be exchanged for equivalent fractions as appropriate in order to build up a complete circle (for example, 2 quarters may replace a half).

■ **Inventing a game.** Encourage the children to devise their own games using this mat and fraction pieces – laminated card pieces are useful.

Circle Resource Sheet

Name...

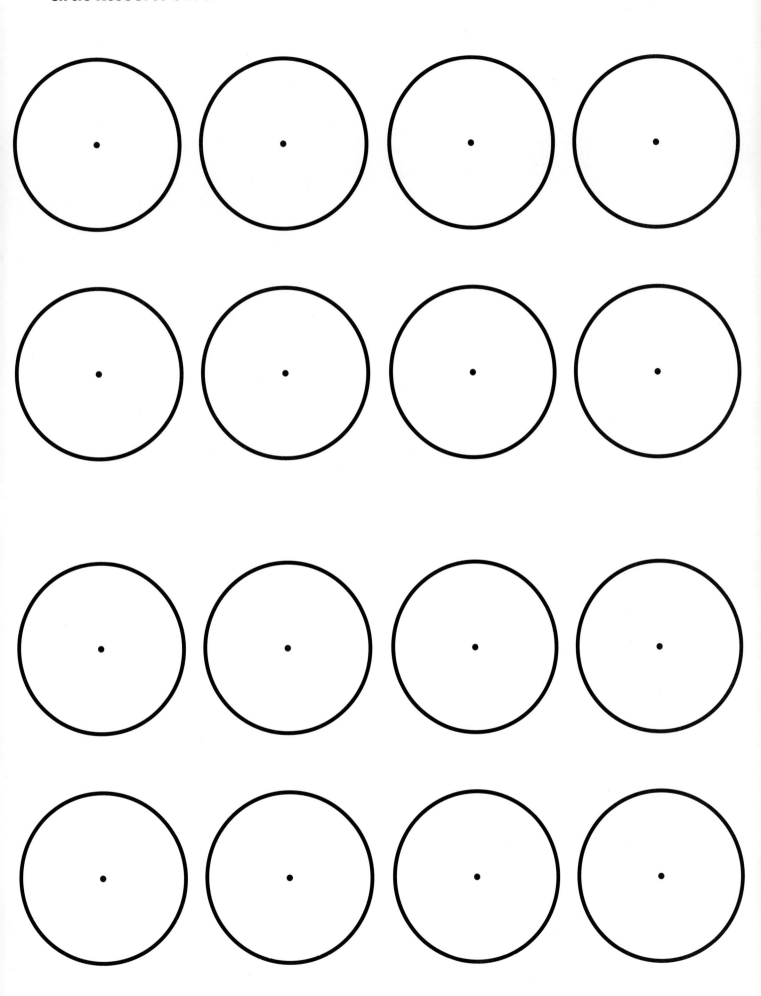

Theme park

Mathematical concepts

Number recognition, counting, sets, more than, less than, number pattern, number investigation, early addition, early multiplication, vocabulary (ordinal number position); shape pattern, shape investigation.

Description of the mat

The mat has been designed as a language stimulus. The centre contains four main features, each of which may be used independently to provide focus for discussion.

The helter skelter shows 3 children in the windows, 4 coming down the 'slide'. There are 5 windows, 3 with faces, 2 empty. The design includes triangles, squares and rectangles.

The big wheel is based on an octagon and lots of features of 8.

The 8 carriages each have room for two people; half (4) are full, 4 have one person only, none are empty.

The roller-coaster has a track wide enough to write inside and a series of 10 connected carriages each containing a number of passengers. Carriages are coloured in a repeating pattern: red, green, yellow.

The boating lake has ten boats, numbered 1 to 10 in the following colours.

Three green (8, 10, 7), three red (5, 4, 1), two yellow (6, 3), 2 blue (2, 9).

The boats have different numbers of occupants: four are empty (1, 2, 7, and 9), three have one person (3, 5 and 10), one has two people (6), one has three people (4) and one has four people (8).

The border can be used to explore pattern and shape. It has a design using just circles, squares and triangles, alone and in combinations with part patterns along the sides so children can focus upon each side to look for the pattern.

Useful resources

Large counters, a 1–6 dice, large and small circles, squares and triangles, Trains resource sheet.

Teacher's notes

■ **General discussion.** The mat is very detailed and there are lots of things to find. It is important to focus on particular features for detailed discussion once the children have had a chance to discuss what they have seen generally.

▲ **Simple number work.** Begin by counting the various features.
Point to and identify the numbers 1 to 10 on the boats.
Count the number of passengers in the various boats.

● **Ordinal numbers.** Point to and count along the carriages to find ordinal position. Ask, for example, 'Show me the third carriage; what colour is it?'

■ **Comparing.** Encourage discussion involving comparison.
'Which boat has the most/least passengers?'
'How many boats have 3 passengers?'

▲ **Adding.** Ask questions to stimulate addition, for example, 'How many people are in yellow boats?' (red carriages, etc?)
'Draw me 3 boats with 3 people in each.' This will be the start of actual recording. Introduce simple symbolic people.

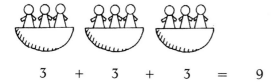

● **Number bonds.** You could produce a simple resource sheet to suit the activity. For example, pairs of boats will produce totals up to 8: a boat holds a maximum of 4 people. If you have two boats how many people might you have inside? Draw all the options.

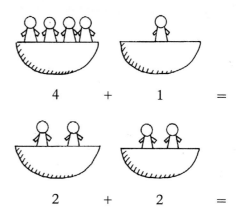

This activity will really show which children approach problem solving logically with an ordered strategy and which tackle the task randomly.

■ **Recording.** Children could be encouraged to devise their own recording methods as you tell a story about the boat trip. Tell the children to draw the picture as you tell the story.

On Sunday Mary, Jim, Sacha and Floyd decided to go to the boating lake. They were given a green boat with a number 8 on the side. Four boats were not being used. There were two yellow boats, one with two people, the other with only one person...

That story describes the mat but you can make one up to include any numbers you want. This could form an assessment activity to test knowledge of number to four and number names as well as understanding of position words. You can easily introduce other elements you want to assess.

There are five boats moored side by side.

The middle boat is number 6, the first is number 3, the last is number 10.
The boat on the left of number 6 is number 4 and the boat between numbers 6 and 10 is number 8.
Which boats are out? (1, 2, 5, 7, 9)

▲ **Extension – to encourage problem solving.**
There are possibilities here for you to challenge the brighter child. Ask:
What would happen if?...
How many people would be needed to fill all ten boats? (40)
How many people are there if half the boats are empty, and half are full? (20)
There are 30 people and half the boats are full. How many people are in the other boats. Can you find several ways?

The questions may vary in level of difficulty and detail. Encourage children to generate their own questions.

Using the resource sheet

■ **Number patterns.** The blank trains could be numbered in order using numbers 1 to 10 or number patterns such as 2, 4, 6, 8, 10... or 3, 6, 9, 12 ...

You could write in some numbers on a copy before duplicating, and ask children to fill in the missing numbers.

▲ **Repeating patterns.** The trains can be coloured in a pattern, such as red, yellow, red, yellow, etc.

• Number bonds. Draw a total of, say, 12 people in the train. How many are in each carriage? Alternatively, a collection of people could be drawn along the train then counted and totalled.

● **Odd and even.** The wheels can be numbered 1 to 20 then coloured with odd and even in different colours.

■ **Recording.** The children could use the sheet to record verbal instructions, such as, 'In the first carriage there are 2 people; in the next there is only 1 person; ... The last carriage is empty.'

Using the border

■ **General discussion.** Discuss the shapes shown.

• How many large/small circles are there?
• Are there more large squares or large triangles?
• Cover the small circles using large counters.
• Use vocabulary such as above, below, inside, outside, left, right, large, larger, small, smaller.

▲ **Combinations.** Develop the idea of shape combinations and talk about the designs. Count each of the single shapes then the combinations.

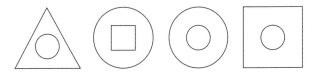

Ask children to investigate what other designs could they produce using the two shapes each time, one inside the other. The two shapes can be the same. Introduce the element of colour and it becomes really challenging. Simplify or extend as appropriate.

● **Shape family: a game for 2 to 4 players.** You need a 1–6 dice, a different coloured counter each and a tray of circles, squares and triangles, both large and small. Get the children to find items that could be used, such as coins, Polydron and Clixi.

This is a collection game. Players agree before starting what the winning collection will be, for example, 6 circles and 4 squares (2 large, 2 small) or 2 each circles, squares and triangles, irrespective of size. This can create a lot of discussion and requires knowledge and understanding of the range of shapes included in the border. Notice there are lots of circles and squares, but no small triangles.

Place your counter on one of the 4 corner stars to start. Take turns to roll the dice and move clockwise round the board. Each time you land collect either 1 or 2 shapes from the tray.

If you land on a plain triangle, collect one triangle. If you land on a small circle inside a triangle, collect one small circle and a triangle.

Play continues until one of the players collects the agreed shape family.

This game can be played over and over again with different rules.

Extension activities

■ **Simple algebra.** Introduce simple algebra using the shapes to represent values, like a simple code. Combinations score as the total. For example

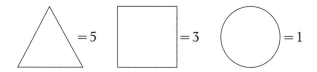

- Discuss the possible totals that may be made.

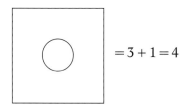

- Cover all the shapes with a total of 2.
- Cover all the shapes with a total of 4.

Once the children are confident manipulating the totals, use a dice 1–6 to generate the numbers for a game.

▲ **Shape cover up: a game for two players.** You need 10 coloured counters, for each player. The aim of the game is to be the first to use up your 10 counters.

Take it in turns to roll the dice and then cover a box containing a shape combination to match your score.

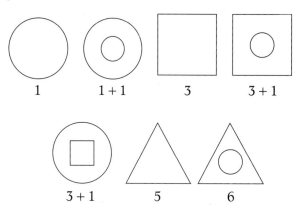

Once all the shapes of a particular value are covered anyone rolling that number will miss a turn. There are more of some numbers than others so you will not always find a shape to cover.

Play continues until one player uses up their counters.

● **Shape number bonds.** Make a set of master cards showing the three shapes with their values underneath.

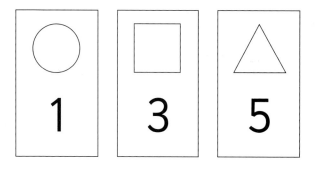

Use these shapes to make different totals: for example, you can make six with:
6 circles,
2 squares,
1 square and 3 circles
or 1 triangle and a circle

Now try 8, 10, etc.

Trains

Name...........................

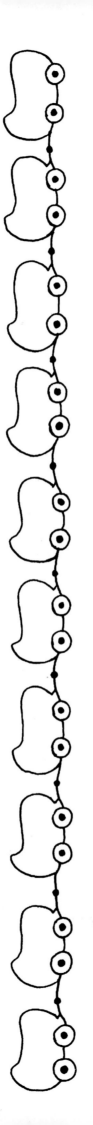
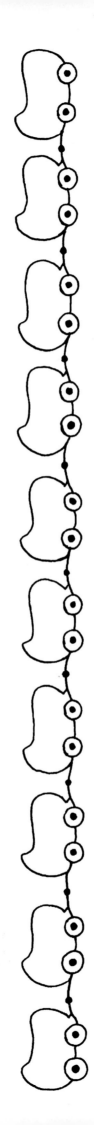
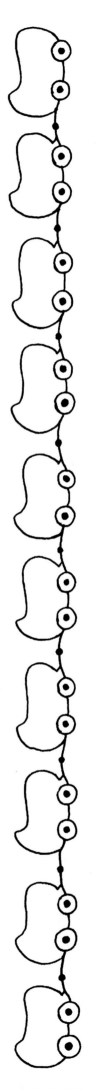

Boots and shoes

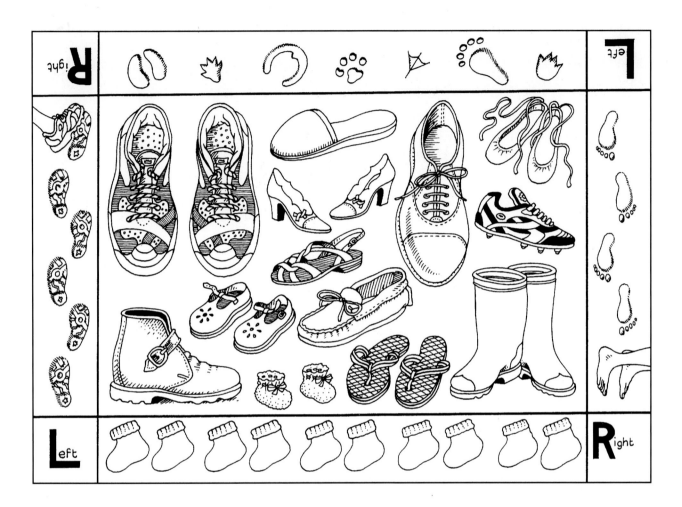

Mathematical concepts

Number, odd/even, pairs, multiplication by 2, counting in 2s, exploring subtraction; matching, sorting, comparison, large/small, left/right, opposites.

Description of the mat

This mat has been designed to generate discussion, for sorting, matching and counting. The collection of footwear shown provides opportunity for sorting, studying left and right, and comparing size.

The footprints in the border provide a good opportunity for work relating to size. The five pairs of socks in the bottom border can lead into work on pairs and simple multiplication (1 pair = 2 socks, 2 pairs = 4 socks ...) and develop into a simple investigation.

Useful resources

A collection of boots and shoes in various sizes; socks for sorting into pairs; laces of various lengths for measuring; Socks resource sheet.

Teacher's notes

Using the centre

- **Preliminary discussion.** This mat has 7 pairs of shoes (14) plus 6 odd shoes making a total of 20 shoes to count. You could count in twos to produce a simple number pattern. Then introduce other counting systems as appropriate. Talk about who would wear the various types of shoe and boot shown. Put a marker on the footwear with buckles/laces, or on those worn in warm weather/wet weather/indoors/outdoors, etc.

- ▲ **Investigate 20.** Use these twenty items of footwear to investigate 20.
  Cover up shoes to represent subtraction, eg
  cover the pairs: $20 - 14 = 6$
  cover the shoes with buckles: $20 - 3 = 17$

- ● **Sorting shoes.** Make a collection of boots and shoes. Order these into:
  - matching pairs
  - order of size, largest to smallest
  - sets of colours, black, red, brown, blue, ...
  - sets by style (eg summer sandals, laced shoes, party shoes, ...)

  You can do similar activities with a collection of socks.

Using the border

- **Preliminary discussion.** Look at the prints of shoes on the left border. Look at the shoe, and match it with one from the actual collection. Talk about the animal prints across the top border. Discuss what type of animal/bird may have made the print. (from left to right: cow, hedgehog, horse, dog, duck, bear, fox)

- ▲ **Left and right.** Focus left and right using the border corners for pairs of children opposite each other.

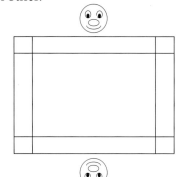

Give the children instructions for building towers of bricks or counters to provide practical experience of using left and right. For example

Put 6 yellow cubes on the left, 3 on the right.
Put 2 orange cubes on the left, 5 on the right.
Put 4 green cubes on the left, 1 on the right.

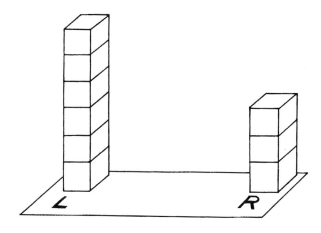

Which side has the most orange, most yellow, ...?
Which side has the least green, least yellow, ...?
Which side has the most cubes?

- ● **Using the socks.** There are 10 socks which can be numbered 1 to 10. They are in pairs to provide opportunity to introduce counting in pairs: 2, 4, 6, 8, 10. You could write on the socks with an spirit pen, or on the resource sheet:

1 pair   2 pairs   3 pairs   etc

You could also use them for work to reinforce odd and even numbers, and group them into various sets.

- **Number work.** The resource sheet could be used for work with pairs of numbers. For example,

Insert a number into each sock to produce identical pairs. Find each total.

10   12   20

Put a number (1–10) into each sock so that each total is, say, 9.

Practical follow-up work

- ■ Make footprints. Compare and measure for size.

- ▲ Measure lengths of stride.

- ● Compare length and width of feet.

- ■ Draw around feet and compare.

- ▲ Create a shoe shop. Try on shoes for size. Find shoes that are too small, too big, too narrow, just right.

- ● Collect some shoes. Draw around the sole then compare the shape and size.

- ■ Explore the number of steps needed to walk along a metre stick.

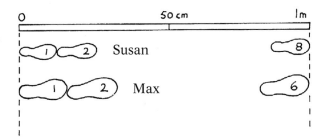

Susan needs 8 steps to cover 1 metre. Max needs only 6 steps. Who has the longest shoe?

- ▲ Develop the work with left/right using turns to left and right in logo.

Socks

Name..